Contents

KV-176-994

Introduction
Acknowledgements

Quizzes
Wine – Elementary   1
Wine – Intermediate   4
Wine – Advanced   7
Wine – France   11
Wine – Germany   14
Wine – Italy, Spain, Portugal   17
Wines – Others   19
Beer in General   22
Beer in Particular   24
Vodka   27
Aperitifs and Such   29
Gin   31
Liqueurs   33
Rum   35
Cognac and Armagnac   38
Brandy (One Step Down)   40
Distillation   43
Minor Spirits   45
Scotch Whisky i   47
Scotch Whisky ii   50
Whiskies and Whiskeys   52
Port   54
Sherry   56
Madeira, Marsala and Others   58

Cocktails and Mixed Drinks   60
Inventors and Inventions   63
Pousse-Café I   66
Pousse-Café II   68
Pousse-Café III   70
Alcohol and Your Interior   73

Answers   75

Introduction

Although drink is a contentious subject – I have seen grown men close to blows over whether you should or should not bruise the mint in a Mint Julep – there are a lot of facts connected with it, some well known, some less so, and some on the fringes which may have their own appeal. (What would you probably have been offered to drink at the court of Attila the Hun? Mascara – where might you find yourself drinking some? How is Freddie Fudpucker remembered?) And although tastes differ here at least as widely as in any other field, there is consensus too – you and I may well not see eye to eye over which Tuscan red is our favourite, but we would have to agree with everybody else that the finest brandy in the world is Cognac.

All in all there is a great deal of ground to cover, even if the enterprise makes no claim to be comprehensive and limits itself to giving samples of A and interesting bits of B. To reel such things off one after another on the 'Did You Know?' principle would be boring for the writer and indigestible for the reader. An obvious answer was a series of quizzes. I love trying to answer such things myself if the subject is right, in the hope of scoring points of course, and impressing the other fellows with my genius, but at least as much to acquire information offered in a teasing way. I may turn out not to know the year of Schumann's birth – it was 1810, I find – but I would be quite tickled to learn it from the answer to somebody's question 17 (b). So I have been prodigal of information, some of it not specially useful information, quite a lot of it historical, vaguely literary, and concerned with the origins of words. This last, I think, appeals to a fair number of those who speak our extraordinary language.

Besides information there is inevitably opinion, sometimes others', more often mine. Drink, as I have said, is not a field where all agree, and an objective essay on it, even in such a form as this book, would be a poor thing. At the same time I have tried not to let those opinions of mine affect the nub of question or answer. I praise or query or am rude parenthetically, from the sidelines.

Whether or not readers will feel the same, compiling this questionnaire suited me down to the ground. It put together in a unique and pleasurable way my abiding partiality for the subject, the attraction of a kind of writing new to me and an outlet for my starved didactic instinct, and was great fun to assemble.

There are a few trick questions and other dodges in what follows, but it would spoil things to be more specific.

Acknowledgements

Those familiar with the works of Burton Anderson, Richard Boston, Michael Broadbent, John Doxat, David A. Embury, Patrick Forbes, Michael Jackson, Hugh Johnson, Tony Lord, R. J. S. McDowall, Brian Murphy, Pamela Vandyke Price, Cyril Ray, Jan Read, Jancis Robinson, Frank Schoonmaker, Serena Sutcliffe, Ben Turner and Roy Roycroft, and 'Trader Vic' will soon see that I am too, and have mercilessly and gratefully plundered them. But of course I remain responsible for everything said here.

Abbreviations
COD – Concise Oxford Dictionary
OED – Oxford English Dictionary
Q – quiz
q – question
a – answer

Quizzes

Wine – Elementary

Short of demanding to know why red wine is called by that name or what champagne is, I have made this quiz as easy as possible. But I advise you to deign to answer it and pile up marks for what may be thin times ahead. So straight to business without lingering over explanations that wine is often kept in bottles, drunk out of glasses, etc.

1 Wines vary in many ways, of which perhaps the most important is the amount of alcohol they contain. What percentage of alcohol would you expect to find in:
  (*a*) a light wine
  (*b*) a strong wine?

2 When a wine is said to lack body an adverse criticism is obviously being made, and everyone knows what is meant without necessarily being able to explain just what 'body' is. Can you?

3 Some wines can be told apart by the bottles they come in. Describe briefly the characteristic shape of
  (*a*) the Burgundy bottle
  (*b*) the claret bottle (by the way, what exactly is claret?)
  (*c*) the Chianti bottle?

4 A fluid ounce (UK) is one-twentieth of an Imperial pint. State:
  (*a*) the number of fluid ounces in a standard wine-bottle

1

Answers on page 77

(b) the metric equivalent of that amount in terms of litres.

For good measure (ha ha ha) explain

(c) what an American means by a fifth of liquor.

5 What is meant when a bottle of wine is said to be corked?

6 The following are all types of – what?
Cabernet Sauvignon Muscat
Riesling Gamay Sylvaner.

7 Three well-known French wines. Briefly describe each (e.g. 'a dry white wine') and name the region where it is made; extra marks for further precision. In this and the following two questions the main or usual product is meant, so if a lot of red and a little white is made the answer is 'red'.
(a) Barsac
(b) Sancerre
(c) Beaune.

8 Three Italians. Proceed as before, but naming the places will probably be harder, so double any marks you get in this way.
(a) Asti Spumante
(b) Valpolicella
(c) Frascati.

9 Three from – elsewhere. Double bonuses again.
(a) Rioja
(b) retsina
(c) *vinho verde*.

10 It has been said (no doubt untruly) that some show-off Japanese businessmen buy the most expensive bottle of claret they can find, take it home and stand it on the mantelpiece. Apart from the showing-off, what is ill-advised about this practice?

Wine – Intermediate

Here is a further selection of miscellaneous questions about wine, some historical or literary, some modestly technical. I excluded with reluctance several that appeared in my first draft, such as the one asking for a definition of a wine-table – a semi-circular or horse-shoe-shaped table with metal wells for bottles and ice and sometimes a revolving wine-carriage. The drinkers sat round the longer edge. Good to know, perhaps, but unenlivening to be asked about.

1 Which famous poet referred repeatedly to the 'wine-dark sea', and what is the significance of that?

2 Can you give a date for the first mention of wine in (a sort of) English?

3 What was the revolutionary seventeenth-century discovery that made possible wine as we know it today?

4 In the 1860s and later a new species of aphis or aphid or plant-louse attacked and laid waste many European vineyards. Give its name and say how the situation was (partly) retrieved.

5 Climate, weather and soil are all obviously important in the first stage of wine-making. Describe a fourth factor.

Answers on page 78

6 Is *vin rosé* given its colour by leaving the (black) grape-skins in the must (fermenting juice) a shorter time than for red wine, or by just mixing red and white wine?

7 When the wine-grower has got his grape-juice ready for fermentation, how does he cause that process to start?

8 Nearly all sweet white wines are made by checking fermentation, so that some of the sugar stays as sugar instead of becoming alcohol. How does the wine-maker do that?

9 Red wine goes with red meat, white with fish and white meat. True or false?

10 What was the precious trade secret bequeathed by the dying wine-maker to his assembled family?

Wine – Advanced

It is impossible that, among the many thousands trying to solve these quizzes, there should not be some few who know more than I do about one or other of the topics covered. Nowhere is this more likely to be so than in the field of wine. For reasons too boring to go into, my expertise there has never been of a very high order. In the present quiz particularly, some questions may appear too easy, others too difficult to offer a sporting chance of a solution. Well, there we are.

1 Let us imagine a wine-tasting, nothing elaborate, just someone out to try an unfamiliar wine. What information can he gain by noting the appearance of the wine in the glass before him?

2 I will not ask you what the taster might notice when sniffing at the wine in his glass, because you cannot be trusted not to start using words like flinty or forthcoming or dumb to describe various smells, so just stick to mentioning a couple of olfactory signs that all is not well.

3 You are undoubtedly aware that acids are most important in the production of wine, being essential to fermentation, also required in the finished article to impart bite or crispness. But can you name the principal acids naturally found in grapes?

7

Answers on page 80

4 You know no less well that the presence of sufficient tannin is equally necessary, in red wines at least. (Some writers refer to tannin as 'tannic acid', how properly I have no idea.) What is its contribution?

5 Identify:
   (*a*) Chablais
   (*b*) Misket
   (*c*) Muskat-Ottonel.

6 Identify:
   (*a*) Inferno ·
   (*b*) Rust
   (*c*) Buzbag.

7 Assign the following to their countries:
   (*a*) Tassenberg
   (*b*) Schramsberg
   (*c*) Brauneberg
   (*d*) Kahlenberg
   (*e*) Steinberg.

8 Assign the following to their countries:
   (*a*) Quincy
   (*b*) Malmesbury
   (*c*) Worcester
   (*d*) Bellingham
   (*e*) Llanarth.

9 Assign the following to their regions or districts:
   (*a*) Chiroubles
   (*b*) Coulé de Serrant
   (*c*) Domaine de Mont-Redon
   (*d*) Scharzhofberger
   (*e*) Frecciarossa.

10 Assign the following to their villages within the Bordeaux region:

    (*a*) Château Branaire-Ducru
    (*b*) Château Durfort-Vivens
    (*c*) Château Pedesclaux
    (*d*) Château Cos-d'Estournel
    (*e*) Château Marquis-d'Alesme.

Wine – France

To find a generalization about French wines that should be both true and unhackneyed would take a very long time. Their pre-eminence continues, though not as before. Thirty years ago, the wine drunk at any kind of serious meal had to be, in the UK at least, a French wine – Chianti was okay at Luigi's. Now, half a dozen other countries are competing at the lower and middle levels, where French performance seems to have fallen off. But at the heights no doubt they still lead. If Australia or California ever catch up, we shall have to go there to find out. Can you see them sending us their best stuff?

1 Some wine is produced in almost every part of France, but certain regions are regarded as outstanding. List the top six – not in order of merit, which would be a hopeless undertaking.

2 What do these letters stand for and what is their significance?
    (*a*) AOC or AC
    (*b*) VDQS.

3 Recently the French have been pushing products called *vins de pays* in the UK. What is the significance of this name?

Answers on page 81

4 Perhaps unwillingly, the wine-drinker finds himself picking up small bits of French. For an easy five marks, translate the following:

(a) *brut*
(b) *frais*
(c) *pétillant*
(d) *mousseux*
(e) *blanc de noirs.*

5 In certain humid conditions, white wine-grapes are attacked by a disease that causes them to concentrate their sugar and eventually produce the marvellous sweet wines of Sauternes. What is the disease called, and what brings it about?

6 The traditional champagne-glass is rather like a small saucer on a stem. Experts dislike them, moaning that they make the bubbles escape too fast. Whatever view you take, say how the thing is supposed to have been given its shape.

7 How did the bubbles get into the champagne in the first place?

8 Has all champagne got bubbles in it?

9 Some champagne is put into freakishly large bottles, larger than the magnum or double bottle, though the practice is probably on its last legs. Give the names and respective contents of these monster bottles.

10 It would be hard to think of a wine-producing country that did not make at least one wine from the Muscatel grape. They are all of course sweet dessert wines. Or are they?

Wine – Germany

German wines are highly respected for their quality, the average of which must be unequalled elsewhere. They are so good that it seems a pity to spoil them with food. Despite strenuous efforts by the trade, this remains the German view. Outside and largely inside the small wine-growing region in the south-west of the country, what washes down the pig's knuckles and dumplings is beer, from one or other of the 1,400-odd breweries in the Federal Republic. The time for a hock or moselle is mid-morning or after dinner, here no less than there.

1 What do these letters, seen on wine-labels and elsewhere, stand for and what is their significance?

(*a*) QmP

(*b*) QbA.

2 The German vineyards are often said to be the northernmost in continental Europe. This cannot really be so, as Holland is said to produce some wine, though I cannot discover (or imagine) where the Dutch vineyards are. Anyway, if you drew a latitudinal line westwards from the northern tip of the German ones, where would it hit England? Or would it miss altogether? Hands off the atlas.

3 Until the seventeenth century, just after Shakespeare's time, Englishmen called wine from the Rhineland 'Rhenish'. Then they started switching to 'hock'. Where did the new name come from?

4 German wines are grouped today as hocks and moselles or mosels. I undertake to tell them apart before they are even poured out. Am I vainly boasting?

5 There is a variety of wine called *Eiswein*, not often seen even in Germany and very expensive. Explain what it is.

6 The sweet dessert wines of Germany are very highly esteemed and are thought to be surpassed only, if at all, by those of Sauternes. The same disease of grapes is at work in both cases. Give its German name.

7 Now an easy one. Name the odd man out:
Rheinhessen   Rheingold   Nahe
Rheingau   Rheinpfalz.

8 Define the following:
(*a*) *schaumwein*
(*b*) *sekt*
(*c*) *liebfraumilch*
(*d*) Riesling
(*e*) *tafelwein*.

9 If *Trockenbeerenauslese* signifies the sweetest wines of Germany, and it does, how can *Trocken* alone indicate a dry wine, as it does?

10 There is a vineyard and a wine in the Rhineland named after one of our monarchs and another in the moselle country whose name commemorates the fact that the personal physician of another strongly recommended it. Can you identify them, i.e. the vineyards/wines? Clue: the two monarchs were related.

Wine – Italy, Spain, Portugal

Although wines from these three countries are drunk in the UK in fair quantities, those from Spain and Portugal increasingly so, not a great deal is generally known about them. In the case of Italy, lack of knowledge may be something to do with the amiable semi-chaos of its labelling habits. As regards Spanish wines, to me what may need explaining is less the prevailing ignorance about them than the prevailing readiness to drink them. Wines from Portugal, on the other hand, quite different from those of Spain, have long struck me as mysteriously underestimated for their merit and variety.

1 Nobody deserves a mark for knowing that *'vino secco'* is Italian for 'dry wine'. It may be a little harder to arrange the following in ascending order of sweetness, starting with a word meaning 'bone-dry'.
    amabile   asciutto   abboccato   dolce   pastoso.

2 What do the letters DOC, seen on a wine-label, stand for and what is their significance?

3 Some Italian wines have the term *'classico'* attached to their name, as Chianti Classico. Does this mean anything substantial?

4 What about *'riserva'* similarly used?

5 Name the odd man out:
    Verdicchio   Vermentino   Frascati

Answers on page 85

6 Few of those reading this will be unaware that '*viño blanco*' is Spanish for 'white wine'. The following are used to indicate other kinds of wine. Name them.

(*a*) *Espumoso*

(*b*) *rosado*

(*c*) *corriente*

(*d*) *tinto*

(*e*) *de mesa*.

7 The Spaniards like ageing their best wines, especially the reds, in oak barrels. What is the most noticeable effect of this on the flavour?

8 A lot of Spanish red wine perhaps understandably finds its way into Sangria, the cold punch. Give its essential ingredients; quantities not required.

9 There are some very decent table wines, both red and white, made in a region of north Portugal. Can you say their collective very brief name?

10 What is the wine speciality of the town and region of Setúbal not far from Lisbon?

Wines – Others

'Others' is not a very sonorous or evocative term for anything, certainly not wine. But some such expression is hard to avoid when the produce of five continents is under discussion. No disparagement is intended. Strange to think that one or other of the 'others' will sooner or later be producing the first wines in the world to give Lafite and Yquem a run for their money.

1 You probably know a lot about Tokay or Tokaji, the famous dessert wine of Hungary, its amber colour, the volcanic soil it comes from, all that, but can you define the following?
   (*a*) Tokay Aszu
   (*b*) Tokay Eszencia
   (*c*) Tokay Szamorodni.

2 Another wine from Hungary is probably more widely known today than Tokay, namely Egri Bikavér. What sort of wine is it, and what is it called in the UK?

3 What is Schluck?

4 Cyprus has been rapidly improving its wines of late. Its best-so-far dry red has a name most inappropriate to an export to the UK. What is that name?

5 The wines of the USA are expanding their overseas markets by leaps and bounds, but they are not yet well

19

enough known in this country for a detailed question on them to be fair. So just name a few states of the Union at present making wine of some quality.

6 Which South American country produces the most wine, more than all the others put together?

7 Distinguish between English and British wine.

8 Australian wines have had a great and deserved success over here in recent years, but are individually known only to a small circle as yet. So have a go at the date of the first wine-harvest there. As a special concession you may look up the date of the first settlement, or alternatively allow yourself ten years' leeway.

9 The South Africans have also been doing well in the UK, but the same applies. If you want to find out more, whom do you ask? (Not much of a quiz question, perhaps, but you might like to know the answer.)

10 Name the odd man out:
Japan   China   Afghanistan   India   Canada.

Beer in General

Until about ten years ago nobody in this country seemed to know anything about beer. The drinks it was proper to know about came down pretty much to wine, fortified wine and brandy. Now all that is changed, and beer has become a field not just of knowledge but of aggressive knowledgeability too. I suppose this has its good side, and certainly a decent glass of draught beer is not the rarity it was in many places. The trouble is that there are so few pubs where one can endure to stay long enough to drink it.

1 In most contexts, 'ale' and 'beer' are names for the same thing, but the terms were far from interchangeable in previous ages. Can you say what the difference was?

2 What is or was porter as applied to beer?

3 What was the original meaning of the term 'stout' as applied to beer? What gives it its distinctive dark colour?

4 The brewing process begins with the malting of barley. Explain this and say what it does.

5 A later stage in the brewing process involves wort. What do you understand by this term?

6 Hops were probably first used in brewing as a preservative, and they clarify the beer too. But they also have an important effect on the flavour. Describe it.

7 We all know, assuming that we can take in what we read, that yeast is used in the making of beer (and wine), but what exactly is yeast and what is its function?

8 What does sediment in a bottle of beer normally indicate?

9 We sometimes see on a pub beer-pull an announcement that the stuff is 'cask-conditioned draught beer'. Give the shorter and more usual expression.

10 What are the advantages of pasteurizing beer?

Beer in Particular

This is likely to be a difficult quiz for uncommitted beer drinkers. What is still our national drink draws less attention and interest than wine, a foreign importation. A man who will be able to tell you unhesitatingly that Margaux is in the Médoc is more than likely to look quite blank if asked where Ruddles Bitter comes from. [Rutland, in fact Oakham, once the county town, now said to be part of Leicestershire.] But general knowledge should be of some service here.

1 About 30 per cent of the beer sold in GB nowadays is lager. Everybody knows this blanket term for vaguely continental-style lively beer, but what is the significance of the name?

2 Pilsener beer or Pilsener lager is a popular type of beer in many countries. Where does the name come from?

3 Diät Pils from the Holsten brewery in Hamburg has been very successful in GB. Although plenty of British drinkers believe it to be a weight-watcher's beer, it is actually rather more fattening than the average brew. True or false?

4 Where can you:
   (a) legally get a Fix
   (b) find Time for a Tiger?

5 Which famous expedition ended up in the wrong place for lack of beer?

6 Various lagers originating abroad are brewed under licence in GB. Name the parent country of:
   (*a*) Stella Artois
   (*b*) Kronenbourg
   (*c*) Carlsberg
   (*d*) Heineken
   (*e*) Vaux.

7 Name the Big Six brewers in GB.

8 Here are five outstanding English beers. Give the home town of each.
   (*a*) Greene King Abbot
   (*b*) Gale's Prize Old Ale
   (*c*) Brakspear's Pale Ale
   (*d*) Adnam's Bitter
   (*e*) Fuller's ESB.

9 Identify:
   (*a*) bock
   (*b*) kvass
   (*c*) saké
   (*d*) erdbeer
   (*e*) lambic.
   One is odd man out.

10 Four London pubs have given their names to districts, reputedly, at least. Can you name them?

Vodka

It was in the early 1950s that vodka began its amazing progress to popularity in the Western world, doubly amazing when you consider what a dull drink it is, no good neat, unsuitable for cocktails. Its only respectable role is as a kick-provider in what would otherwise be soft drinks; I once recommended its sparing use as a stiffener for the cold punch at a Darby and Joan Club party. These remarks of course apply only to Anglo-American vodka. Many Eastern ones are flavoured, often with what may seem bizarre substances like cayenne pepper or chocolate, but even the straight ones have some character.

1 What does the word 'vodka' mean literally?

2 What is the drink made from?

3 When and where was vodka first made? Approximate answers permitted.

4 Name the leading firm of vodka-producers in Imperial Russia. Not an unfair question, as you will see.

5 Name the Polish vodka of which every bottle contains a blade of so-called bison grass, supposedly brought from the forests of east Poland where the surviving beasts are said to roam.

27

Answers on page 90

6 There are Russian and Polish vodkas distilled out at 96 *per cent* alcohol, and legally too. What is the reason (or excuse) for this?

7 Most people know the delicious (but rather indigestible) Bloody Mary with its tomato-juice, Worcester sauce and other juices and spices stirred up in vodka, but can you describe:
(*a*) a Bullshot
(*b*) a Hotshot
(*c*) a Bloodshot?

8 How can you tell a White Russian from a Black Russian?

9 One of the least offensive drinks made with vodka is the Moscow Mule – vodka, ginger beer and lemon-juice traditionally served in a copper mug. In what circumstances did it come into being, and what is the historical significance of its arrival?

10 Name the famous Russian who, while on a visit to Paris, wrote home to his wife, 'There's only one bottle of vodka left; I don't know what to do.'

Aperitifs and Such

A disagreeable word, aperitif, but eighty years or so after its introduction into English it can surely be considered naturalized and lose its French pronunciation and accent. No native word will do its job; taking its anglicization a stage further and talking and writing about an aperitive is quite inoffensive, indeed admirable as far as it goes, but seems unlikely to catch on. And now, on to the quiz, lest I fritter away what information I have about this, to me, less than wildly exciting province of alcohology.

1 When a waiter or a host mentions an aperitif he means one thing; a man in the drinks trade means another, more specific. Give:
  (*a*) the broad and
  (*b*) the narrow senses of the term.

2 Apart from wormwood and many other herbs and spices and such, what are the main constituents of vermouth?

3 Wormwood and vermouth. Are the two similar-sounding words related?

4 French vermouth is dry, Italian sweet. True or false?

5 What is:
  (*a*) Chambéry
  (*b*) Chambéryzette?

Answers on page 91

6 (*a*) What is the name of the popular mixed drink made from Campari and red vermouth?
   (*b*) What does it become if you add gin?

7 Campari is named after the ancient Roman town of Camparum, where a supposedly health-giving drink was made in classical times. True or false?

8 Angostura is another famous bitters in a completely different style from Campari. The name comes from the place of origin, but it is now made somewhere else. Can you say where? One mark for the general area, an extra one for the precise location.

9 Some brands of bitters are used as pick-me-ups or remedies. Can you name:
   (*a*) an Italian and
   (*b*) a German version?

10 What is the main ingredient that imparts bitterness to bitters and to some other drinks?

Gin

'Drunk for 1d, dead drunk for 2d, clean straw for nothing.' It is apparently compulsory to give that quotation, supposed without any evidence to have come from a notice displayed outside eighteenth-century gin-shops in London, in every book about drink and article on gin. However, it does serve to make the point that gin had for many years a thoroughly unrespectable 'image', not quite lost even today. Like Scotch whisky, and unlike vodka and white rum, gin is associated with people who like drink.

1 Give the derivation of the word 'gin'.

2 Gin has always had a pretty bad press. The very first citation in O E D, dated 1714, refers to it as an 'infamous Liquor' and 'intoxicating' – not just inebriating but fatally poisonous. A later writer called it 'liquid Madness sold at tenpence the quartern' (gill or quarter-pint) in 1839. Can you say who?

3 Not all writers have taken such a harsh view. Which famous poet, asked where he got his inspiration from, replied, 'Gin and drugs, dear lady, gin and drugs'?

4 What is unusual about the flavour of gin compared with that of brandy, whisky and most other spirits?

5 Where and when was gin (probably) first made, and what was its first use?

Answers on page 93

6 What are the basic materials from which gin is distilled?

7 Apart from the advantages of its being the capital, what was it about London that made it an excellent place to set about making gin?

8 What is pink gin? Be specific.

9 How long must newly-distilled London gin be matured in cask or vat before it is ready for bottling?

10 A drink based on gin was drunk by Sir Horatio (later Lord) Kitchener's officers during the campaign in the Sudan in 1898. What was it, or what is it now called?

Liqueurs

This is a wide, vague term embracing drinks made by radically different processes (see q 1). A few years ago one could safely have drawn the generalization that liqueurs were used for drinking after meals. They still are, but what must be a greater quantity finds its way into mixed drinks. Southern Comfort from the US is the example here, allegedly to be seen in company with white wine or even Tequila.

The word itself is a useful shibboleth, separating the good Joes who make it rhyme with 'secure' from the affected persons who frenchify it as 'lee-*cur*'.

1 The Danish drink familiarly known as Cherry Heering and the almost equally famous Kirsch from the upper Rhine region both taste of cherries, but there is a basic difference in their modes of manufacture. State it briefly.

2 Not many liqueurs are based on gin, but Sloe Gin is. I can reveal that it is obtained by steeping sloes (small wild plums) in gin. What is the traditional occasion for serving it?

3 What was the most important result of the battle of Culloden?

4 Name the odd man out:
Grand Marnier   Orange Curaçao
Yellow Chartreuse   Strega   Benedictine.

Answers on page 94

5 Why should a liqueur made from Armagnac, honey and herbs remind me of pelota?

6 What are you supposed to do when a glass of Sambuca, an Italian liqueur made with witch elder-brush (eh?) and liquorice, is served to you with three coffee-beans floating in it?

7 Name liqueurs made with:
    (*a*) mint
    (*b*) apples
    (*c*) blackcurrants
    (*d*) caraway seeds
    (*e*) plums.
Easy. An extra mark for naming the country of origin.

8 Name liqueurs made with:
    (*a*) lemon-tree leaves
    (*b*) arbutus berries
    (*c*) walnuts
    (*d*) naartjies
    (*e*) shaddocks.
Not so easy. Country of origin as before.

9 Liqueurs are often used in cocktails, of which the best-known is probably the White Lady. Give its main ingredients.

10 Who is supposed to have introduced liqueurs into France? (Clue: she came to marry the Dauphin of the day.)

Rum

Rum started in the Caribbean, where the Royal Navy took it up in the early eighteenth century because it kept better than beer and, presumably, made life just bearable. The daily rum ration, to which the seamen's rights were carefully protected, continued until 1970. It – the ration – had been strong and large enough to put the consumer well over the limit permitted to car-drivers, and their lordships no doubt felt that this was unsuitable in the days of guided missiles. The vogue for white and pale rums was getting into its stride at about the same time.

1 Give the derivation of the word 'rum'.

2 Rum is made from various products of the sugar-cane.
  (*a*) What is sugar-cane botanically, i.e. what type of plant is it?
  (*b*) On which islands was it first seen by Europeans?

3 Grog was traditionally a drink of rum and water introduced into the RN in 1740. Whence the name?

4 The rums made in the various islands and in Guyana differ widely, being made by different methods, but all are the same colour when they leave the still. What is this colour?

5 Rum is or was reputedly known as Nelson's Blood. Is there more to this than affectionate metaphor?

  Answers on page 95

6 A Cuba Libre is a drink nowadays made of white rum, Coca Cola and lime-juice (rum 'n coke to unworthy persons), the name meaning 'Free Cuba'. Free from what or whom?

7 White rum, lime-juice and sugar produce a delicious cocktail which could legitimately be called a Rum Sour, but is usually given a more particular name. What is that name, and whence is it derived?

8 Planters' Punch is traditionally made from dark Jamaica rum, lime-juice, sugar and water or soda-water. Can you recite the doggerel rhyme that states the recommended proportions?

9 Apart from the British and Americans, rum-drinking nations include the Australians and the Mexicans, who make their own, and the French, who import theirs – from where?

10 Rum is indeed made in many countries, islands, regions. Which of them is the top producer in quantity?

Cognac and Armagnac

These two are by common consent the finest brandies in the world. To a lot of people they are rather similar, but then a lot of people never get the chance, or just possibly cannot be bothered, to move about among the many and various brands and grades of each and make comparisons. Connoisseurs seem to think Cognac is quite different from Armagnac, and in trying to describe the difference excel even themselves in high-flown writing. The excellent Pamela Vandyke Price admits to having written that the appeal of Armagnac is emotional whereas that of Cognac is intellectual. If you have to go to such heights, or lengths, to distinguish the two, well, perhaps a lot of people are not so wrong after all.

1 As well as being the names of drinks, Cognac and Armagnac are names of places, regions of France. Roughly where are those regions?

2 Again by consent, the product of Cognac is the finer of the two. Name the area within it that produces the best Cognac of all.

3 When do we first hear of something like brandy being made:
    (a) in Cognac
    (b) in Armagnac?
    Roughly.

4 Arrange in ascending order of quality:
VSOP VSTO VO Three Star XO
Cordon Bleu.

5 Which of the following substances may legally be added to Cognac during manufacture?
Neutral spirit Sugar Burnt sugar or caramel
Martinique rum Infusion of oak-chips.

6 Name the odd man out:
Otard Hine Delamain Delaforce Camus.

7 What kind of still is used in the making of:
(*a*) Cognac
(*b*) Armagnac?

8 How long on average should a high-grade Cognac or Armagnac be allowed to mature in bottle before drinking?

9 Is there such a thing as Napoleon brandy?

10 What part of Cognac is said locally to be consumed by the angels?

Brandy (One Step Down)

Nowadays most brandy in this country is drunk either after full-dress meals or for medicinal purposes, and a brandy and soda or brandy and water before or between meals is rarely seen. In the past, however, these diluted versions were very popular and were often served at table alongside wine. On the other hand, some early brandies may well not have been brandies at all, but primitive and no doubt quite vile forms of whisky. The restriction of the term 'brandy' to mean 'distillate of wine' is comparatively recent. Fruit brandies, as plum brandy, pear brandy, distillates from the fruit specified, are considered in Q Liqueurs.

1 What is the derivation of the word 'brandy'?

2 Since, as noted above, 'brandy' used by itself means a spirit made from grapes, one might think that the phrase 'grape brandy' was a tautology. But not so; it has a precise meaning. State it.

3 What do they give you in France if you ask in a bar or restaurant for a *fine à l'eau*?

4 The taste and particularly the aroma of brandy come out in full only if the glass is slightly warmed. What is the approved method of bringing this about?

5 As Dr Johnson famously said, 'Claret is for boys; port for men; but . . .' But what? Exact words, please.

6 'Brandy will do soonest for a man what drink *can* do for him.' Who said that?

7 Of which country can brandy be said to be the national drink?

8 Identify the following:
  (*a*) marc
  (*b*) grappa
  (*c*) weinbrand
  (*d*) bagaceira
  (*e*) pisco.
  One of the five is an odd man out.

9 An Alexander Cocktail is obviously made with brandy or it would not be here. Best made with a decent but not first-rate one. What are the other ingredients, and why is it often called an after-dinner cocktail?

10 Which mode of transport would be most useful to a tax official out to identify the brandy warehouses in a brandy-making centre?

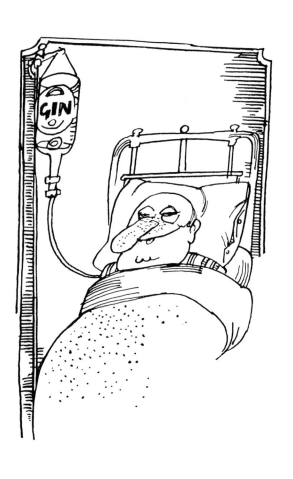

Distillation

The process that gives us spirits or strong drink is very old, but it has been only very recently in comparative terms, from about the time of the first railway systems, that the distiller has had any but the vaguest and most general control over his product. Nowadays distillation is a branch of technology, and yet essential parts of the procedure continue to defy measurement. There is no substitute so far for the stillman's skill and experience.

1 Give a short definition of distillation. (Remember, water can be distilled.)

2 What is the physical property of alcohol that is so useful, indeed indispensable, to the distiller?

3 To obtain a spirit or spirits, the distiller needs as raw material some substance containing alcohol. By what process will this have been produced?

4 It is safe to say that the invention of the still is the sort of thing that happens independently in more than one place. Nevertheless, give the conventional account of the historical beginnings of distillation. (Clue: It may be helpful to read the next question before starting to answer this one.)

5 Proponents of this view often cite linguistic evidence in its support. State it, and evaluate it if you can.

Answers on page 99

6 Outline a more up-to-date proposal about the provenance of distillation. (NB: We are of course interested in distillation less as a technological process than as the source of whisky, gin, etc.)

7 Stills of a type that has not changed in principle since the earliest times continue in use for the production of Cognac, malt whisky, Tequila and other spirits. Name this type and indicate its three basic parts.

8 When a spirit emerges from the type of still just mentioned, it retains a content of substances called congeners or congenerics. What are these, and what are their effects?

9 Many spirits on leaving the still are blended with another liquid which may itself have been distilled. What is it, and what is the purpose of introducing it?

10 Some potable spirits, such as gin and vodka, are said to have been rectified. What is meant?

Minor Spirits

Somebody once said it must be depressing for God to notice that, all over the world he created, his children were drinking spirits in an effort to get away from it, and if I could remember who it was I would have set a question asking who. But the unknown sage was certainly right about the near-universality of the hard stuff, and no one needs to be told about the enthusiasm with which spirits have been taken up by those few races that, like the American Indians, were too backward to have developed them off their own bat.

The description 'minor' refers to geographical distribution and volume, not quality. Akvavit, in particular, is a drink fit for a king, and Aalborg brand is the worthy holder of a warrant to the Danish court.

1 Akvavit or aquavit is the staple spirit of Scandinavia, a very pure distillation from grain or potatoes made like gin and usually flavoured with – what?

2 How are you supposed to serve and drink akvavit?

3 What is Linie Aquavit?

4 Swedish Punsch is not a punch in the ordinary sense of an on-the-spot mixture but a ready-bottled blended drink to be served hot or cold. What is the principal ingredient?

 Answers on page 100

5 Pernod and Ricard, respectively brands of anis and pastis, are two very popular French drinks said to resemble the long-exiled absinthe whose drinkers were portrayed by Degas and Toulouse-Lautrec. What are the two (drinks) made from?

6 Both these drinks are traditionally taken with water in the proportion 5:1. Can you say why, from being clear though coloured liquids, they turn cloudy when the water is added?

7 Elsewhere in Europe there is another popular drink with a strong family resemblance to Pernod and Ricard, in that it too clouds with water. Say where and what.

8 Mezcal and Tequila are both made in Mexico from the fermented sap of a plant related to the American aloe – not a cactus after all, it seems, in spite of what is often said. What is the relation between the two?

9 The best-known Tequila cocktail is the Margarita. I know few more delicious, nor any as productive of aggro. What does it consist of?

10 This quiz is supposed to range widely, so I ask you finally to name the spirit the Tartars of central Asia distil from fermented mare's milk.

Scotch Whisky I

In about a century Scotch has been transformed from a purely local restorative, designed to get a poorly-fed, badly-housed populace through hard days and cold nights, to a major export of the UK, the most widely distributed of all quality drinks and, at its best, the equal of any spirit in the world. Recently its prosperity has been hindered by economic depression and a trend, in the UK and elsewhere, against strong, dark-coloured drinks, but there is still no competitor in sight.

1 The Finance Act of 1969 embodies a necessarily complicated definition of whisky, but its subsequent definition of Scotch whisky is straightforward enough. What is it?

2 The Act also specifies a minimum time the spirit must spend being 'matured in wooden casks in a warehouse' before it is sold. What is that time? Choose from:
  Ninety days   One year   Thirty months
  Three years   Five years.

3 Give the derivation of the word 'whisky'.

4 Most Scotch sold is a blend of malt whisky, made in a pot still, and grain whisky, made in a patent still. In what way is the patent still greatly superior to the pot still?

Answers on page 101

5 Malt whisky is made from malt, i.e. malted barley. What is grain whisky made from?

6 Some malt whiskies are said to have a peaty taste and aroma. Where do these qualities come from?

7 Many factors influence the character of a malt whisky. Perhaps the best known of these is the water, also important in determining the flavour of beer. Name three others known to affect malt whisky.

8 A malt whisky is often listed and labelled as a single malt. What is the significance of this?

9 Most of the malt whisky distilleries of Scotland are in the Highlands. There are, however, three other named areas producing their own types of malt whisky. Enumerate them.

10 Dr Johnson said he had only tasted whisky once in his life, 'for experiment', and added: 'It was strong but not pungent. What was the process I had no opportunity of inquiring, nor do I wish to improve the art of making poison pleasant.' True or false?

Scotch Whisky II

Professor R. J. S. McDowall, the great authority on Scotch whisky, wrote that whiskies 'are almost as numerous and varied as the wines of France', and the more one explores the truer his remark proves to be. Yet all Scotch has one thing in common – it goes badly with anything but water and more of itself, in short it is a bad mixer, a fact that makes its world-wide success surprising as well as splendid.

1 Name the odd man out:
Chivas Regal Glen Grant Glenfiddich
Glenlivet Glenmorangie.

2 In what important way does the chemical composition of a mature whisky, aged in cask for ten or fifteen years, differ from that of a whisky at the end of manufacture but before casking?

3 Blended whisky was well into its stride in Scotland by 1865 or so. The distillers began to cast their eyes on England, where whisky was all but unknown except as the stuff you drank on grouse-moors. What historical accident greatly helped their sales drive?

4 About how many brands of blended Scotch whisky are made?
90 250 800 1,200 3,000

5 What is Atholl Brose?

6 What sort of casks are used for the maturing of malt whisky? ('Wooden' is not a sufficient answer.)

7 Which royal personage is said to have been partial to a half-glass of claret topped up with Scotch? Not impossible to guess.

8 In a blended Scotch, what are the proportions of malt whisky and grain whisky likely to be?

9 From what does Scotch receive its colour?

10 Where is the largest distillery of malt whisky in the world? A precise location is not required. But something of an imaginative leap is.

Whiskies and Whiskeys

Only Ireland, the US and Canada dare put themselves forward as producers of whisky fit to be compared to Scotland. (The first two customarily spell their wares 'whiskey'.) There is a fifth land, however, thousands of miles away from the nearest of the other four, that almost any moment will be pronounced worthy to be put in their league. Irish resembles Scotch in its intractability, not going well as part of any orthodox mixed drink.

1 One of the Irish whiskey distilleries is said to be the oldest in the world. Which and where is it, and what is its most famous product?

2 Irish coffee is a delicious exception to the rule about Irish whiskey's unsuitability for mixtures. Its preparation is not very troublesome, but it becomes virtually impossible in the absence of one commonplace implement. What is it?

3 There are many varieties of whiskey made in the US, of which bourbon is the most popular and best-known and the one usually seen in the UK. Where does it get its name from?

4 What is bourbon:
   (*a*) made from
   (*b*) matured in?

5 A few American whiskeys are known as 'sour mash' whiskeys. What does this signify?

6 The Old-Fashioned Cocktail is the most famous of all those made with whiskey. List its ingredients.

7 Which of the following were whiskey-distillers as well as pursuing other activities?
George Washington   Thomas Jefferson
Walt Whitman   Glenn Miller   John Wayne.

8 Name the odd man out:
Old Grandad   John Jameson   Jim Beam
Old Forester   Wild Turkey.

9 Canadian whisky has been very successful in recent years outside as well as inside its own country. Which of its characteristics is usually thought to be responsible for this?
Strength   Weakness   Purity
Lack of after-effects   Aroma

10 Whisky, so called, is made in dozens of countries, including Argentina, Iran, Tanzania and India. What do these drinks usually consist of, and can any of them properly be called whisky?

Port

The trade in port grew up to meet English demand, and its general character was designed to meet the centuries-old English taste for sweet wines. To this day, many of its great names are English or Scottish – Sandeman, Cockburn, Dow, Croft, Taylor, Graham. The UK no longer holds the position of the world's biggest customer for port, having yielded it to France, where they make no bones about drinking sweet wines before meals. Nevertheless port has held up best in the national drift away from drinks in this category.

1 Port not only comes from Portugal, it comes only from there, in the sense that under our law no wine from any other country may use the name. More precisely it comes from Oporto in north Portugal, whence it gets its name. But where are the vineyards where the wine is grown?

2 Nearly all port is sweet and all of it is appreciably stronger than ordinary table wine. These are the results of a single process in the manufacture. What is that process?

3 Some months after being made, the immature port is moved to a convenient point for ageing, blending and bottling at the shippers' lodges or warehouses. Where are these?

4 Of the various styles of port the most ambitious is vintage port, invented by the British and still drunk by them almost exclusively, though there is a small market in the US. Define vintage port.

5 What happens to a vintage port:
   (*a*) before and
   (*b*) after bottling?

6 Vintage port is traditionally drunk at the end of a meal, either on its own or with cheese. Which cheese or cheeses does it go best with?

7 In recent years the shippers have been drawing our attention to styles of port that lack the 'mystique' of (and are cheaper than) vintage port, but are a cut above the standard rubies and tawnies. Describe:
   (*a*) Late Bottled Vintage Port
   (*b*) Late Bottled Port
   (*c*) Vintage Character Port.

8 Some white port is made and, especially in France, drunk as an aperitif. How is it made? You can be very brief.

9 Port and lemon (fizzy lemonade) is an old char-ladies' drink, and very good it is on a hot summer's afternoon, but few mixed drinks include port. However, there is one, also known of old, that is intended for nothing more dashing than the relief of diarrhoea. What does it consist of?

10 What was the reaction of the so-called three-bottle men to the arrival of port-as-we-know-it (more or less) in the early eighteenth century?

Sherry

Like port, sherry was developed for the English market. In former times its different varieties were drunk as a table wine, before meals, after meals, at mid-morning with a biscuit. Now no longer universally seen at the dinner-tables of the well-off, it often appears in its drier forms as a prelude to a serious meal and as an accompaniment to first courses like smoked salmon, avocado and consommé.

1 Where do sherry the wine, and 'sherry' the word, come from?

2 'A good sherris-sack hath a two-fold operation in it. It ascends me into the brain; dries me there all the foolish and dull and crudy vapours which environ it; makes it apprehensive, quick, forgetive, full of nimble, fiery and delectable shapes; which, delivered o'er to the voice, the tongue, which is the birth, becomes excellent wit. The second property of your excellent sherris is, the warming of the blood; which, before cold and settled, left the liver white and pale, which is the badge of pusillanimity and cowardice: but the sherris warms it and makes it course from the innards to the parts extreme.' Who said so?

3 There are plenty of references to sherris-sack, or just sack, at the period of the above. What does 'sack' mean in this context?

4 'Sherry is dull, naturally dull,' said Dr Johnson, normally quite tolerant of alcoholic drinks (except at the times when he was off them altogether). What had he got against sherry?

5 Sherry is traditionally made by the solera system. Describe this briefly.

6 While sherry is developing in the barrel a thick white layer of yeast forms on its surface. Give its name.

7 Sherry is naturally a dry wine, but some types are sweetened to varying degrees. Arrange in ascending order of sweetness:
   Oloroso   Amontillado   Manzanilla   Fino   Cream.

8 Quite a lot of Fino sherry gets drunk at its place of origin, mostly in half-bottles. Is this thrift, temperance or what?

9 Montilla is a type of wine made about 100 miles from Jerez, very enjoyable and rather like sherry in taste, but with one big difference in its composition. What is it?

10 What is:
   (*a*) a sherry-cobbler
   (*b*) a sherryvalley?

Madeira, Marsala and Others

The fortification – 'making strong' – of wines by adding spirit during or after fermentation is a widespread practice, originally intended as a preservative measure or to cheer up thin wine rather than in pursuit of any kind of quality. But a number of such wines have been highly regarded for many years, though in general the demand for them has fallen off more recently.

1 Madeira, a fortified wine once in the same league as sherry and port, comes from an island of that name in the east Atlantic. What does the name mean, and with what common English words is it connected?

2 Four main types of Madeira are made. The most obvious difference between them is in their degree of sweetness. Arrange in ascending order:
   Sercial   Verdelho   Bual   Malmsey.

3 You come across a satisfactorily old-looking bottle labelled Verdelho 1810. Would it have to be a fake? If not, could the wine possibly be drinkable?

4 Who accused who of selling his soul to the devil on Good Friday last for a cup of Madeira and a cold capon's leg?

5 The best-known Italian fortified wine is Marsala. Can you say where it is made, and name either or both of the famous historical characters who took it up and popularized it?

6 If you frequent Italian restaurants at all, you have probably tasted Marsala without knowing it. How?

7 Name a third fortified wine beginning with M.

8 The great dessert wine from the Rhône, Muscat de Beaumes de Venise, is classified as a *vin doux naturel*. What does this mean?

9 It is common for wine-producing countries to make a sweet red wine comparable with port, in general style as a rule, not merit. A French effort comes from the extreme south of France by the Spanish border. What is it?

10 What is Yalumba Brandivino and where does it come from?

Cocktails and Mixed Drinks

The revival of interest in cocktails is very recent, so much so that that close observer, Cyril Ray, could write in 1977 of 'the passing of the cocktail craze'. Some specialized bars in our large cities had kept them going ever since the 1920s, but the only one to survive throughout in anything approaching general circulation was the Dry Martini. And now, in trendy pubs, blackboards invite you to sample the Harvey Wallbanger, the Tequila Sunrise and other exotica our fathers never knew. For those many who like going or being taken to pubs but dislike the taste of drink, a cocktail may be just the thing.

1 Can you give the true, authentic origin of the word 'cocktail'?

2 Defining a cocktail is something else again, and not easy. Try for a form of words that admits all the examples you can think of – or most of them.

3 Cocktails became very popular in the 1920s, particularly in the US. Can you suggest a reason why this should have happened at that time?

4 The Manhattan is a type of cocktail usually but not always made with bourbon whiskey. Name the other ingredients. (There is more than one answer.)

5 A cocktail is preferably served in a cocktail glass, a medium-sized affair with a stem. The Old-Fashioned Cocktail (see Q Whiskies and Whiskeys, q 6), however, is properly served in an Old-Fashioned glass. Describe this, and give the practical reason for its particular shape.

6 A Collins is a popular mixed drink, especially in the US. It consists of gin (John Collins, sometimes Tom Collins), whisky or another spirit and what else?

7 What is:
    (*a*) Buck's Fizz
    (*b*) Black Velvet?
    And can you name and describe two other potations, (*c*) and (*d*), that also possess the feature shared by the first two?

8 It is no secret that Irish Coffee (see Q Whiskies and Whiskeys, q 2) is made with Irish whiskey. But similar drinks with other alcoholic bases may not be so easy to identify. State what the bases are in:
    (*a*) Caribbean Coffee
    (*b*) Italian Coffee
    (*c*) Monks' Coffee
    (*d*) Prince Charles's Coffee
    (*e*) Roman Coffee.

9 Five traditional mixes. Give the chief ingredients of the following (you may skip the fruit-slices, etc.):
    (*a*) the Gimlet
    (*b*) the Sidecar
    (*c*) the Screwdriver
    (*d*) the Stinger
    (*e*) the Singapore Sling.

10 And five trendy ones:
   (*a*) the Freddie Fudpucker
   (*b*) the Harvey Wallbanger
   (*c*) the Blue Hawaiian
   (*d*) the Piña Colada
   (*e*) the Godfather.

Inventors and Inventions

The really important discoveries in the making of alcoholic drinks, such as the ability to induce and control fermentation, are lost in the mists of antiquity. That particular one was probably made several times over in different places, like the making of fire, another important step in human development. But as soon as technology began to enter into the manufacture of drinks, names and dates start appearing. The first five questions here contain the names of five people who invented or devised or for some other reason are associated with something alcoholic. Say what it was or is in each case.

One or two clues are given, but no really helpful ones.

1 Johan Siegert, a German army surgeon who served in the Napoleonic wars and later with Simón Bolívar the Liberator in South America.

2 Aeneas Coffey, an Irishman, once an excise official, in 1831.

3 Robert Stein.

4 The late Felix Kir.

5 Dr Pierre Ordinaire, in Switzerland, about 1790.

Answers on page 109

Now five questions from the other side of the fence. Say who invented or otherwise had to do with the following:

6 Chaptalization, the practice of adding sugar to grape-must to boost the alcoholic strength of a wine. Very popular with wine-makers in thin years.

7 The *cuve close* (sealed vat) method of making sparkling wine. The manufacturer induces his refermentation in a large vat instead of individual bottles. Widely used outside the Champagne region.

8 The traditional British system of calculating the strength or proof of alcoholic drinks, whereby standard spirits are 70 degrees proof or 70°.

9 Champagne. Not as easy as it may look.

10 The Dry Martini Cocktail. There is no certainty here, but it was *probably* one of the following:

Jerry Thomas Martini Rossi Martini di Arma di Taggia Martini-Henry John Doxat

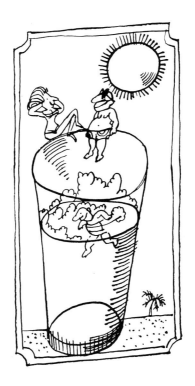

Pousse-Café 1

My French dictionary says a *pousse-café* is a liqueur, my English one says much the same, helpfully adding '[F, = push-coffee]', but the UK Bartenders Guild explains that it consists of liqueurs of different densities poured into a glass one after the other in such a way that they remain separate bands of fluid, and gives a recipe involving Grenadine, Crème de Menthe, Galliano, Kümmel and brandy. I use it as the heading of this quiz to indicate fancifully that the questions here involve different sorts of drink, this one wine, that one spirits, a third something else again. Here and there I hope the question will not directly reveal the category concerned.

1 What, apart from its availability, is the characteristic of the human foot that fits it so well for the making of wine?

2 What is twice a chota peg?

3 If you were to ask for 'a beer' in English at a French café, especially in Paris, what might you very well be given?

4 No substantial authority has ever found drinkable any of the so-called 'cotton gins' of Mississippi and Texas. True or false?

5 In what circumstances might you find yourself drinking Mascara?

6 There is a fearful drink called a Snowball which combines Advocaat, lime-juice and fizzy lemonade or even 7-Up. But Advocaat itself is not bad as a between-meals drink. What is it?

7 Distinguish between Ay and Ahr.

8 The neck label on a bottle of Hungarian Tokay wine may carry the legend '*Aszu* 2 *puttonyos*' or some other number. What is the significance of this?

9 Every serious drinker in this country owes a small debt of gratitude to the French physicist Joseph Gay-Lussac (1778–1850). Why?

10 'People may say what they like about the decline of Christianity; the religious system that produced Green Chartreuse can never die.' Who wrote that?

Pousse-Café II

Here is another miscellany quiz. Whatever answerers may feel about them, setters like the freedom of manoeuvre such arrangements give them. The answer to a wine-quiz question, say, is already partly indicated by its presence there. But here, some legitimate mystification is possible.

1 Name the odd man out:
Beaujolais Villages   Beaujolais Primeur   Beaujolais Gamay Beaujolais   Beaujolais Nouveau

2 What is the largest alcoholic product of Jerez de la Frontera in Spain?

3 It is safe to say that wherever spirits are made, a proportion will be illicitly made. Some of the slang terms for these are widely known. Give three:
(*a*) orginating in UK
(*b*) in US
(*c*) in Ireland.
(You may well think that (*a*) too has US origin.) For bonus marks, guess dates of first recorded use; twenty-five years' leeway allowed.

4 Soda-water was first made as a substitute for naturally gassy spa waters thought to be beneficial to health. But something called Spa water, in bottle, is to be seen today. Where does it come from?

5 What is meant by saying that a bottle of wine is *chambré*?

6 In the production of alcoholic drinks, which country leads in quantity in:

  (*a*) spirits
  (*b*) wine
  (*c*) beer?

7 What soft drink, still very popular as a mixer, was enforced in the Royal Navy in the mid-nineteenth century, and for what purpose?

8 Vintage port and other wines that throw a sediment are traditionally decanted, but in recent years people have been taking more and more to decanting light, clear wines, even whites. What is the purpose of this?

9 Define negus.

10 'It is WRONG to do what everyone else does – namely, to hold the wine list just out of sight, look for the second cheapest claret on the list, and say, "Number 22, please".' Who wrote that?

Pousse-Café III

1 Name the Roman god of wine, and his Greek counterpart.

2 You still occasionally see mead, which may well be the oldest of all fermented drinks and certainly goes back to the beginnings of the English language, about AD 700. What is it made from?

3 And what is metheglin, once supposedly the national drink of Wales?

4 Wine and spirits are often matured in wooden casks. Which wood has proved to be best for this purpose?

5 Give:
    (*a*) the approximate date when and the probable place where wine was first made.
    Also the approximate dates of its introduction to:
    (*b*) Greece
    (*c*) France
    (*d*) England.

6 On average, by and large, etc., how many bottles of wine are made from the fruit of a single vine – or how many vines are needed to produce a bottle?

7 A certain stage in the making of wine and beer involves what is known as racking. Define this process.

8 Every good host, perhaps every civilized person, ought by rights to have a bottle of sparkling water in his refrigerator. While you may assent to the general proposition, do you consider it true or false?

9 Name the odd man out:
  (*a*) whisky-jack
  (*b*) brandy-snaps
  (*c*) Scotch snaps
  (*d*) Danish snaps
  (*e*) gin-wheel.

10 'No animal ever invented anything so bad as drunkenness – or so good as drink.' Who wrote that?

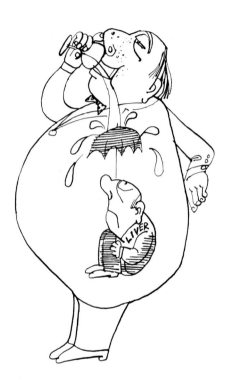

Alcohol and Your Interior

There can be few subjects of general interest more ridden with folk-lore and superstition than the physical effects of alcohol and the measures taken to limit and alleviate them. We have all met the man who says he actually drives better after a few drinks than when cold sober. Many people believe that black coffee – why *black* coffee? – sobers you up, whereas all it does is keep you awake. On the other hand, the consensus that liqueurs are tricky has good sense in it.

Remember that doctors disagree on these matters quite as much as on any others, so some of the answers here must fall some way short of total scientific objectivity. There is no way to measure drunkenness, after all, nor, thank heaven, a hangover.

1 'Winter warmers' are a recognized category of drink, but does alcohol warm you? – it certainly makes you *feel* warm. Elucidate.

2 We are often warned against mixing our drinks, especially 'grape and grain', i.e. wine/brandy and beer/whisky. Doing so supposedly:
   (*a*) makes you drunk
   (*b*) gives you a hangover.
How much truth is there in these assertions?

3 Quantity of intake is an obvious factor in drunkenness. So is food, or rather lack of it. Can you suggest others?

 Answers on page 114

4 Apart from a large alcoholic intake, what else seems to cause or aggravate hangovers?

5 Most of us have learnt better by now than to call alcohol a stimulant; it is, we keep hearing, a depressant. Does it inevitably cause a state of depression?

6 Excessive drinking is a cause of cirrhosis of the liver. True or false?

7 Excessive drinking, especially of port, is a cause of gout. True or false?

8 Apart from the unthinkable resort of drinking less, is there any stratagem that will limit the intoxicating ravages of alcohol?

9 What is and what is not good for a hangover is such a personal matter, and so much influenced by suggestion, that any ruling must be tentative, but try to give a balanced, educated view of:
    (*a*) two beneficial things
    (*b*) two useless or harmful things.

10 Although a small amount of alcohol daily is beneficial to health, there will always be some support for teetotalism – a terrible word, many will think. What is its origin?

Answers

Answers

Wine – Elementary

1 (a) 8–10 per cent (b) 13–15 per cent.

2 The proportion of grape-products as opposed to water-content. A wine of good body is a thick wine in this sense.

3 (a) Cylindrical, with sloping shoulders.
(b) Cylindrical, with squarer shoulders. Claret, traditional UK term for red wine from Bordeaux region. Now used also for other wines of the same general type.
(c) Traditionally, long neck, rounded body, straw jacket and base. An extra mark for noting that a lot, an increasing amount, of Chianti turns up nowadays in a bottle similar to (b).

4 (a) 26⅔. Not an obvious quantity but it seems about right.
(b) Three-quarters of a litre or 75 cl. The French and others must have thought it was about right too.
(c) (A bottle containing) a fifth of a US gallon, smaller than the Imperial at 128 fl. oz. compared with 160. When a tiny difference in the size of the US fl. oz. is taken into account, the fifth emerges at 46.5432 cu. in. as against the standard wine-bottle's 46.2458. So the Americans must also have thought it was about right.

5 That it has acquired an unpleasant smell and taste from a mould in the cork. Very rare today.

6 Wine-grapes. There are at least 1,000 different varieties. Many wines, from Alsace, California, Australia, etc., are known by the type of grape used. They are called varietal wines.

7 (a) *Sweet white from Bordeaux. In Sauternes district.*
(b) *Dry white from Loire valley. Central France.*
(c) *Dry red, (district of) Burgundy. East-central France.*

8 (a) *Sweet white sparkling Muscatel from Piemonte in the north west.*
(b) *Dry red from Veneto, north-central, near Verona.*
(c) *White, usually dry, some semi-sweet and sweet, Latium, near Rome.*

9 (a) *(Chiefly) dry red, from Rioja region in north Spain.*
(b) *Dry white flavoured with pine resin, from Greece (Attica).*
(c) *'Green wine', i.e. young, immature wine, red and white but usually white in UK, dry, with a slight sparkle, from north Portugal.*

10 *The cork of an upright bottle will eventually dry out and admit air, rapid fluctuations of temperature will injure the contents and daylight will, in the case of a red wine, turn it brown. But not drinking it is worse than any of that. One such offender, father of a daring and ingenious son, is supposed to have decided eventually to drink his 1959 Château Haut-Brion after all and found his mouth full of red ink.*

Wine – Intermediate

1 *Homer. His use of the phrase suggests that wine had become a familiar part of eastern Mediterranean life by 700 BC at latest.*

2 *About AD 700, in the Old English epic poem 'Beowulf'.*

3 *The cork. Wine could now be kept and matured in the bottle instead of sitting (and frequently going off) in the barrel.*

4 *'Phylloxera vastatrix' – 'dry-leaf devastator'. Retrieved by grafting European vines on to relatively immune root-stocks from the eastern US. But e.g. in 1981 one-third of German vineyards were still affected.*

5 *The type of grape used or principally used, given increasing emphasis in recent years. Crosses are becoming common.*

6 *Both, naturally; e.g. Tavel rosé by the first method, some pink champagne and some cheap still wines by the second. Then, of course, there is the 'vin rosé' your host has created half an hour before your arrival by mixing the undrunk red and white from yesterday.*

7 *Years ago he just hung about and let the natural ambient yeasts do it, but nowadays he usually kills them off and puts in his own pure strain, perhaps with a little added heat for encouragement.*

8 *He can chill the must or add brandy or sulphur dioxide to deaden the yeast, or strain the must to get the yeast out.*

9 *True! Which does not mean to say that red will not go with chicken or pork, or that individual preferences are somehow bad.*

10 *'Wine can also be made from grapes.' You may specify a French, Spanish, etc., wine-grower according to where your last lousy bottle came from.*

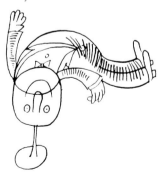

Wine – Advanced

1 *Having satisfied himself that the wine is not cloudy – a sign of trouble – he studies the colour. With reds, a purple tinge indicates a young wine, brick-red a more mature one. With whites, lightness, perhaps with a greenish tinge, indicates youth, straw colour is standard, yellow may well mean age, but depth of colour also indicates degree of sweetness. Any hint of brown in red or white may foreshow bad quality.*

2 *A woody or metallic smell suggests a fault in the cask. A vinegary smell calls for no great powers of reasoning. But other acid smells are harmless, and chemical smells from disinfectant agents often go away after a few minutes. All the same, I would avoid (where socially possible) any wine with an unexpected smell, not to speak of a disagreeable one.*

3 *Tartaric and malic. There may be traces of citric and more than a dozen other acids.*

4 *It may sharpen the flavour, though not everyone cares for its bitterness or famed 'mouth-puckering' effect. 'Plenty of tannin' is a fashionable commendation. Also a preservative, lengthening the period of improvement in bottle. Often artificially introduced into poor wine.*

5 *(a) Mostly dry white wine – some red – from the district of Chablais near Lake Geneva (Switzerland).*
(b) Bulgarian Muscat. You hardly need telling that this is the generic name for sweet white wines made from the Muscat or Muscatel grape.
(c) The same, from Romania, Yugoslavia, etc., named after the variety of Muscat grape.

6 *(a) Red wine from an area so named in northern Italy. (Paradiso is next door.)*
(b) White wine, dry and sweet, some red, from the Rust area in east Austria.
(c) The standard red produced by the Turkish state wine industry.

7 (a) *South Africa*
  (b) *US (California)*
  (c) *Germany*
  (d) *Austria*
  (e) *Germany.*

8 (a) *France*
  (b) *South Africa*
  (c) *South Africa*
  (d) *South Africa*
  (e) *Wales (Dyfed).*

9 (a) *Burgundy (Beaujolais)*
  (b) *Loire*
  (c) *Rhône*
  (d) *Mosel (Saar)*
  (e) *Lombardy.*

10 (a) *Saint-Julien*
  (b) *Margaux*
  (c) *Pauillac*
  (d) *Saint-Estèphe*
  (e) *Margaux.*
  All of these four names are within Haut Médoc.

Wine – France

1 *In alphabetical order:*
  Alsace Bordeaux Burgundy Champagne The Loire
  The Rhône

2 (a) *'Appellation (d'Origine) Contrôlée'. Means that the wine comes from where the label says it comes from. Also some assurance that it has been properly made and is up to strength.*
  (b) *Similar, but not so strict about area and other things.*

3 A 'country' or local wine coming from a general region. Inferior to the other two, with nothing especially authentic or esoteric to them. Worth trying for curiosity's sake, says Hugh Johnson. Well yes.

4 (a) Completely dry, unsweetened (of champagne). But very little wine so marked is in fact totally without added syrup.
(b) Cool, chilled, not ice-cold.
(c) Slightly sparkling, with a 'prickle'.
(d) (Fully) sparkling, but never applied to champagne. One of the minor airs that overpriced stuff gives itself.
(e) White wine made from black grapes. This is theoretically possible if you whip the skins out the moment the juice is removed, but in practice such wines are pale pink.

5 'Pourriture noble' or noble rot, the result of attentions of the fungus 'Botrytis cinerea'.

6 From the shape, but surely not the size, of Marie Antoinette's breasts. I find this story tempting but implausible.

7 Well, because after a few months in store each bottle has yeast and sugar added, causing the famous second fermentation with resultant bubbles.

8 By no means. Some of the wine, not worth giving the expensive treatment described above, is marketed in its original still form. I have met people who say they like it. There are still reds too, of which the best is supposed to be Bouzy.

9
Jeroboam	4 bottles	Salmanazar	12 bottles
Rehoboam	6 bottles	Balthazar	16 bottles
Methuselah	8 bottles	Nebuchadnezzar	20 bottles
Sennacherib	10 bottles		

10 There is one French exception, Muscat d'Alsace, bone dry but with all the rest of the grape still there, a remarkable experience. Sadly, André Simon found it underbred. Oh well.

There is an intruder in the answers above, a fact offered as a plain fact that is not a fact at all. You will find the solution on page 115.

Wine – Germany

1 (a) 'Qualitätswein mit Prädikat', quality's-wine with title or mark. Official designation for top-grade wine that must not be chaptalized (have sugar added to boost the alcohol).
(b) 'Qualitätswein eines bestimmten Anbaugebietes', actually, or quality's-wine of a definite cultivation-territory, in other words of a named wine-growing region. Good wine, but may be chaptalized.

2 Like much else, not easily discoverable from a modern atlas, but the line from Bonn, which is about right for the northernmost German vineyard, passes through or near Bournemouth and Exeter, which incidentally is north of at least four modern English vineyards.

83

3 *From the name of the local port of Hochheim on the river Main, whence most or some of it was presumably shipped.*

4 *Not this time. Hocks come in brown bottles, moselles in green.*

5 *Ice-wine, made from frozen grapes with the ice, i.e. water content, taken out, and so very heavy and sweet, also good, though not the best Germany can do, it appears.*

6 *'Edelfäule', the exact translation of noble rot or 'pourriture noble'. A less regular visitor to the Rhineland than to Sauternes.*

7 *'Das Rheingold' is of course the preludial opera of Wagner's 'Ring' cycle, and the Rheingold also is or was an early-morning express train from the Hook of Holland to Milan. The other four are denominated wine-producing regions of the Rhineland.*

8 *(a) Foam-wine, i.e. sparkling wine, lower grade.*
(b) Sparkling wine, higher grade, or 'Qualitätsschaumwein' if you prefer.
(c) Almost meaningless term for all-right, nothing-special hock. Well defined by COD *as 'mild white Rhine wine'. Legally a* QbA, *which says something about* QbAS.
(d) The best and commonest German grape. Also used for wines from Alsace, Austria, California, Australia, etc.
(e) Table wine. Equivalent to 'vin ordinaire'. A blend of German wines and those of other EEC *countries. 'Deutscher Tafelwein' indicates a blend of German wines only.*

9 *Quite easily. 'Trocken', like 'dry', can mean at least two things. 'Trockenbeeren' are dry, i.e. withered, nobly-rotten, sugar-concentrating grapes. 'Trocken' on its own equals 'sec'.*

10 *Königin Viktoriaberg (Queen Victoria-hill) and Bernkasteler Doktor, the doctor in question being Edward* VII*'s.*

Wine – Italy, Spain, Portugal

1 *'Asciutto'* (bone-dry), *'pastoso'* (off-dry), *'abboccato'* (lightly sweet), *'amabile'* ('amiable', a touch sweeter), *'dolce'* (sweet).

2 *'Denominazione di origine controllata'*, controlled designation of origin. Result of belated (1963) Italian attempt to follow the French AOC example and regulate descriptions and methods. No assurance of quality as such. A higher category is supposedly on the way.

3 Yes, something. It means the wine comes from a reputed best area within the larger area indicated by a DOC.

4 This refers to age. Barolo Riserva and others are three years old, but many named wines have no such grade.

5 Barolo is a red wine, one of Italy's best, from Piemonte in the north west. The others are whites.

6 (a) sparkling
   (b) rosy, pink
   (c) 'current', ordinary, like 'vin ordinaire'
   (d) red
   (e) 'of table', denoting a table wine. (A mesa in Arizona etc. is a table-land.)

7 A flavour of vanilla is imparted to the wine. Some people like this; I find it intolerable.

8 Ice, fresh fruit, sweetness, a kick, bubbles – you can do sweetness and kick together by using a sweet liqueur, or sweetness and bubbles together with fizzy lemonade. Oh, and wine, which after all need not be Spanish.

9 Dão, rhyming with 'cow' but nasalized by the conscientious.

10 Moscatel de Setúbal, a fortified dark-white dessert wine made from the muscat grape and redolent of Victorian elevenses. They do a nice red table wine round there too.

Wines – Others

1 (a) *Standard Tokay, with added 'aszu' syrup from 'nobly rotten' grapes.*
(b) Even sweeter version, low in alcohol, supposedly life-saving 'essence', very rare today. Hugh Johnson persuaded them to give him a swig out of the barrel in the State cellars at a place called Tállya.
(c) The heavy natural wine minus the 'aszu'.

2 *A good full-bodied red table wine that goes down well with pizzas, stews, oxtail, shepherd's pie, chili con carne, etc. Bull's Blood is the name.*

3 *An Austrian wine for swilling, reputedly enjoyable. Not to be confused with schlock, Yiddish American for 'rubbish'.*

4 *Othello. Well, Shakespeare's Othello had a horrible time in Cyprus. Iago's deadly plot against him started with a drinking-session, at which Cypriot wines were presumably on offer.*

5 *California (of course), New York, Oregon, Washington, Idaho, Ohio. Take note that vineyards have been planted in Texas.*

6 *Argentina. But Chile probably leads in quality.*

7 *English wine is made from grapes by proper methods and is perfectly serious, though a bit marginal. British wine is imported as grape concentrate from nameless places, re-hydrated and fermented, finally blended and given a brand-name. In some cases, raisins are probably the nearest things to grapes it has ever seen.*

8 *1790/91, which does sound a bit soon after the founding of the first settlement in 1788. They brought vine cuttings from Rio de Janeiro and the Cape – where they had had wine for 100 years before that.*

9 *The South African Wine Farmers' Association. Tel: 01-734 9251.*

10 *Canada is in North America. The others are in Asia. (All five produce some wine.)*

Beer in General

1 *Ale was made from fermented barley without added flavour, beer was treated with hops. In the UK beer was a novelty of the fifteenth century.*

2 *A type of dark beer apparently first brewed for, or popular with, London porters. Recently revived after long abeyance. Also see next answer.*

3 Strong. 'Stout porter' was the full expression, and what was once called an extra stout porter still flourishes. The colour of stout comes from the roasted barley used.

4 Steeping the barley in water causes it to germinate and convert its insoluble starch into soluble starch.

5 The infusion of malt which is boiled, hopped, and fermented into beer. The word rhymes with Bert.

6 Hops confer bitterness on the brew to balance the inherent slight sweetness of the malt content.

7 The Latin name, 'Saccharomyces', 'sugar-mushroom', tells the story. Yeast is a substance consisting of minute fungous organisms that produce fermentation, in the present case converting the sugars in the wort into alcohol and carbon dioxide.

8 That the beer is still fermenting, is a 'natural' beer, unpasteurized.

9 Real Ale. 'Cask-conditioned' is the jargon of brewers, who are nervous of the term Real Ale because they probably make unreal ale, i.e. keg, as well.

10 Beer is pasteurized by heating it and so killing yeasts and bacteria. It will now not change any further. The advantages of a consistent, stable product are obvious. The process is of course – by definition – frowned on by Real Ale lovers, but bottled and canned lagers as we know them would be impossible without it.

Beer in Particular

1 'Lager' is German for warehouse or store. A lager beer is kept in store for up to three months to settle and mature.

2 From the town of Pilsen (Plzen) in West Czechoslovakia, where the first light-coloured lager was made in the last century. Pilsener Urquell is made there and exported to GB and elsewhere ('Urquell' = original source).

3 True. It has quite high alcohol and therefore calories. Not for dieters in the slimming sense but for those on a diabetic diet. And for beer-drinkers.

4 (a) Greece. From the brewery called that, a fair shot at the name of the German brewer, Füchs.
   (b) Malaysia and Singapore, a Pilsener lager. The phrase is the title of a novel by Anthony Burgess.

5 That of the Pilgrim Fathers, who were bound for Virginia, but landed at Plymouth Rock, 'our victuals being spent, especially our beer'.

6 (a) Belgium
   (b) France (Strasbourg)
   (c) Denmark
   (d) Holland
   (e) England – Vaux Breweries, Sunderland. Sorry, but the name was irresistible.

7 Allied Breweries, Bass, Courage, Scottish and Newcastle, Watney, Whitbread.

8 (a) Biggleswade and Bury
   (b) Portsmouth
   (c) Henley-on-Thames
   (d) Southwold
   (e) London.

9 *(a) In Germany, a strong type of beer, in France, a weak one.*

(b) A type of Russian drink made from bread, beer of a sort.

(c) Japanese rice beer. So describable from the mode of manufacture, not the end result.

(d) Odd man out – German for 'strawberry'.

(e) A type of Belgian beer made from wheat.

10 *The Angel, the Royal Oak, the Swiss Cottage and the Elephant and Castle. The last name, by the way, is not a corruption of 'Infanta of Castile'. The inn-sign obviously showed an elephant carrying a castle, which was the regular fifteenth-century term for a small wooden fighting-tower fitted to an elephant's back.*

Vodka

1 *'Little water' or 'waterlet', from Polish/Russian 'voda', water. No doubt a Slavic jest. But note that Russians particularly are prone to the use of diminutives, and in practice will ask for 'vodochka', 'waterletkins'.*

2 *It varies. Theoretically, vodka is a type of uncoloured grain whisky or pure spirit of grain, and it regularly is that in the US and officially in the USSR. In the UK, often a molasses spirit filtered through 'activated' charcoal, and unofficially in the USSR anything available – potatoes, beetroots, nuts, sawdust, etc.*

3 *Eighth-century Poland, they say, but this was probably a distillation of wine, and so a form of brandy. For what would nowadays be called a vodka, eleventh- or twelfth-century Poland, more likely.*

4 *Smirnoff. The modern Western product derives from a member of the original family, who originated in the Polish city of Lvov, now incorporated in the USSR.*

5 *Zubrowka. Horrible muck according to me, though other Polish vodkas are first-rate.*

6 *They are designed for winter drinking in extreme northern latitudes, where anything weaker would freeze. (Does that mean you are supposed to drink them out of doors?)*

7 (a) *Vodka, beef consommé, lemon-juice, Worcester sauce, lightly iced, a warmer or reviver.*
(b) *The same, gently heated.*
(c) *As (a), but featuring tomato-juice half-and-half with the consommé.*
(d) *An invention of my own for a bonus, the Raging Bull – vodka, lemon-juice and Worcester sauce in a mug of Bovril.*

8 *By the colour. A White Russian Cocktail has vodka and Kahlua Mexican coffee liqueur mixed with cream floating on top, the Black Russian omits the cream. But either is to be avoided by sensitive persons.*

9 *In 1946 in a place called the Cock 'n Bull (a suitable name, you may feel) in Los Angeles a man with a lot of unsold vodka met a man with a lot of unsold ginger beer. A third man, brought in later, had a lot of unsold copper mugs. The success of their joint venture was the beginning of the success of vodka, first in the US, later the UK and elsewhere.*

10 *Peter the Great, in 1716. He took a close personal interest in these matters and invented an improved still.*

Aperitifs and Such

1 (a) *A pre-prandial drink supposed by convention to stimulate the appetite, such as white wine, dry sherry and most of the drinks in this quiz.*
(b) *A branded drink, also called a wine aperitif, in the vermouth style, such as Dubonnet and Punt e Mes.*

2 *Inferior white wine, a little grape spirit or sugar syrup, artificial colouring (red, rosé and sweet white vermouths).*

3 *Our word 'vermouth' comes from the French word 'vermout' which is a frenchifying of the German word 'wermut' which is cousin to the medieval English word 'wermod' which got changed to 'wormwood' because the herb was formerly used in medicine to get rid of intestinal worms, or quite possibly 'wermod' got changed to 'wormwood' because it sounded better and they used it for worming merely because it was called that. So yes, but distantly.*

4 *Once a valid distinction, showing healthy disrespect for the literal fact that the famous Martini Rossi dry vermouth was made in Italy. Now, pedantry on one side and ignorance on the other have rendered it unsafe. False, then.*

5 *(a) A classy white vermouth from the French Alps.*
(b) The same, coloured pink and flavoured with wild strawberries (and therefore with a whiff of whitewash to my taste).

6 *(a) An Americano*
(b) Negroni.

7 *False: it was invented about 1870 by a Milan café-proprietor called Gaspare Campari.*

8 *The Caribbean – Port of Spain, Trinidad.*

9 *(a) Fernet Branca*
(b) Underberg.

10 *Quinine. Such drinks were and often still are thought to have tonic and prophylactic virtues.*

Gin

1 *Perhaps an abbreviation of 'geneva' from Dutch 'genever'* = *'gin', following Old French 'genèvre' after Latin 'juniperus'* = *'juniper', the shrub or low tree whose berries are used in flavouring gin. The form 'geneva' arose from confusion with the name of the Swiss city. I think it more likely that 'gin' is an abbreviation of the English word, of which 'giniper' and 'ginnuper' are early spellings.*

2 *Thomas Carlyle. That Germanic capital should have given it away.*

3 *T. S. Eliot, at a women's luncheon club in the US in the 1950s. He may have been thinking of Byron's remark, 'Gin and water is the source of all my inspiration,' another playful allusion to gin's disreputability.*

4 *The flavour comes from flavourings, substances added to a pure spirit, principally juniper but also coriander and usually cassia bark and orris root, whatever they are. In contrast, the flavour of brandy and whisky comes ultimately from the grape and grain they are made from.*

5 *At Leiden in Holland in the seventeenth century, for medicinal purposes – like every other tipple in the book. Gin was supposed to be beneficial to the urinary system, and English gin is perhaps still taken in moderate quantities to alleviate gout.*

6 *Dutch or Hollands gin is made from malted barley, maize and rye. The English distillers are rather evasive. Grain, they helpfully say, also 'vegetable matter', also, less often, molasses. But all the original flavour is taken out anyway.*

7 *Because of the excellence of its springs or wells, such as Clerkenwell and Goswell. Water is a most important constituent of alcoholic drinks. Or was – the statement is less true today, with the distiller or brewer in control of the chemistry of his water-supply.*

8 *Gin and Angostura bitters – score a quarter of a mark. For specifying Plymouth gin – half a mark. For confining the bitters to just a few drops – three-quarters. For leaving it to the drinker's taste – a full mark.*

9 *No time at all. 'You can make gin in the morning and drink it in the afternoon,' as they used to say.*

10 *Pimm's No. 1.*

Liqueurs

1 *Briefly, and broadly, Heering is a sweetened spirit flavoured with cherries, Kirsch is an unsweetened fruit brandy or 'white alcohol' distilled from a mash of cherries.*

2 *At the meet before a fox-hunt, where it forms the stirrup-cup.*

3 *Well, the defeat of the Stuart cause, but the next most important was probably that after it Bonnie Prince Charlie is supposed to have given the recipe for Drambuie to one of his supporters as a gesture of gratitude before departing into exile.*

4 *Orange Curaçao, the generic name for a liqueur flavoured with orange-peel and orange in colour; the others are brands, in fact Grand Marnier is a brand of Orange Curaçao.*

5 *Because both Izarra liqueur (green and yellow varieties) and the game of pelota belong to the Basque country.*

6 *Set light to it, apparently. There will not be much combustion and the result, which chars the coffee-beans slightly, is quite drinkable (and crunchable).*

7 *(a) Crème de menthe (France).*
(b) Calvados (France). Only half a mark for Applejack (US).
(c) Cassis (France).
(d) Kümmel (Holland, Germany).
(e) Mirabelle (France), Quetsch (Germany), Slivovitz (Yugoslavia, Czechoslovakia).
The above is not a complete list.

8 *(a) Kitró (the Greek islands of Naxos and Ios).*
(b) Medronho (Portugal).
(c) Eau de Noix (France).
(d) Van der Hum (South Africa). The naartjie is related to the mandarin and tangerine.
(e) Forbidden Fruit (US). The shaddock is related to the grapefruit.
The above is not necessarily a complete list.

9 *Cointreau, gin, lemon-juice. White of egg too if you want a fizz.*

10 *Catherine de Medici of Florence.*

Rum

1 *Not certain. Once thought to be an abbreviation of the word 'rumbullion', which might have meant 'uproar', but there seems to be no real evidence of this. Some derive it from Latin 'saccharum' = sugar, but again no written record shows it happening.*

ANSWERS to page 35

2 *(a) A type of giant grass.*
(b) The Azores. Columbus brought cuttings to the West Indies on his second voyage.

3 *'Old Grog' was the nickname of Admiral Edward Vernon (from his waterproof grogram boat-cloak). To limit drunkenness he ordered the men's rum ration to be watered and issued in half-portions of a gill each twice a day. The equivalent of three pub doubles of 90° spirits at eleven o'clock in the morning is still not a small drink.*

4 *'White' or transparent. The darker rums gain their colour from the oak they mature in or from caramel, flavourless burnt sugar. Rum seems to have been artificially coloured in the first place to suit the Navy, which could not afford to risk having on board a strong spirit which the eye could mistake for water.*

5 *Possibly. They say that after Trafalgar the Admiral's body was brought back to England in a cask of rum.*

6 *Imperial Spanish rule, after the Spanish-American war of 1898. With the US occupying forces came Coca Cola, then a comparatively new drink (first sold 1886).*

7 *The Daiquiri. From the place in Cuba where US marines landed in 1898 (see last answer). A duller story gets it from a tin or nickel mine whose manager's butler thought up the drink.*

8 *One of sour, two of sweet, three of strong, four of weak, i.e. water or soda. The so-called American formula reverses one and two, three and four.*

9 *From the Caribbean, principally the island of Martinique. Saint James rum, or rather 'rhum', is very fine, offered alongside Cognac in Paris restaurants.*

10 *Puerto Rico. Bacardi set up its base there when Castro confiscated its Cuban property and now outsells all other brands of spirits in the US.*

Cognac and Armagnac

1 *Cognac, half-way down the Atlantic coast; Armagnac, further down and further in, not far from the Pyrenees.*

2 *Grande Champagne. Nothing to do with the bubbly-producing part of east France, though that is the same word, meaning 'grassy plain' or 'open country' (obsolete English 'champaign').*

3 *(a) Early seventeenth century*
   (b) Early fifteenth century.

4 *These are just manufacturers' labels, but Three Star is the basic grade, which even connoisseurs will not mind you putting soda or other mixers in. Next come* VO *(Very Old) and* VSOP *(Very Superior Old Pale), with* XO *(Extra Old) and Cordon Bleu somewhere in front. The initials of these English words appear throughout the trade, indeed chalked on the barrels in the blending-houses in Cognac itself, a satisfying reminder of our long grip on the trade.*

   A VSTO *gives a different kind of lift. The Very Short Take-Off aircraft was the ancestor of the jump jet.*

5 *Sugar, up to 2 per cent.*
   Burnt sugar or caramel, up to 2 per cent.
   Infusion of oak-chips, no limit, but not a thing you do much. Or talk about much.

6 *Delaforce is a firm of port shippers. The others are Cognac houses.*

7 *(a) A pot still, used for two successive distillations.*
   (b) A unique type of continuous still.

8 *Five minutes is plenty. No spirit improves in bottle.*

9 *Yes and no. A few bottles may survive from that period, would presumably fetch high prices as relics, but the contents would probably be off (and see last answer). Some firms use the term today merely to indicate a high grade, along with such phrases as 'Grand Réserve'.*

10 That which evaporates while the spirit is in cask, the equivalent of several million bottles a year. No way of controlling this has been found which does not damage the brandy.

Brandy (One Step Down)

1 Formerly brandwine, brandy-wine, from Dutch 'brandewijn' = burnt, i.e. fired, i.e. distilled, wine. The Dutch had a lot of influence on the early Cognac trade.

2 Unsatisfactory, illogical, and firmly established trade term in U K and U S for French brandy made outside the Cognac and Armagnac regions.

3 Quite likely a stare of pretended incomprehension, but on a good day a glass of the above with water. In a classy place you might get Cognac.

4 In the hand or hands. Experts get very cross about the use of spirit-lamps and such.

5 '. . . he who aspires to be a hero must drink brandy.'

6 Dr Johnson, immediately after the above. On another occasion he said, 'He who drinks until he becomes a beast gets away from the pain of being a man,' which is hardly funny at all.

7 South Africa. Something like half the national spirit production and consumption is brandy. But cane, a pure spirit made from molasses, is catching up.

8 The odd man out is (c). Weinbrand is a type of German spirit made from wine, the equivalent of French grape brandy. The others are all made by distilling the debris of skins, stalks and pips left in the presses after making wine.
  (a) is the French version, properly 'eau de vie de marc'. The debris itself is the 'marc', or tread (from the verb marcher).

(b) Italian. The word means 'clamp' or 'vice'. Also the name of California spirits of this type.

(d) Portuguese. The word means 'rope-wax'. Humorous deprecation, no doubt.

(e) Peruvian. Sometimes the debris is that of Muscatel wine. Pisco brandy dates back to the early seventeenth century.

9 *Brown Crème de Cacao and cream. Well, it would obviously take away your appetite, if you had one.*

10 *A helicopter. A black fungus forms on the roofs, encouraged by the fumes coming up from below.*

Distillation

1 *The COD defines 'distil' as 'turn to vapour by heat, condense by cold, and re-collect (liquid)'. These are the three essential stages.*

2 *It vaporizes at a lower temperature than water, permitting the separation of the two in the still.*

3 *By fermentation, the product of which will have been the wine used to make brandy, the beery mixture that issues in whisky, etc.*

4 *It was discovered by Arabs, brought into Spain by Moors some time after AD 1200 and thence diffused over Europe.*

5 *Two key words are derived from Arabic: 'alcohol' ('al kuhl', the essence) and 'alembic' ('al inbik', the still – 'alambic' is modern French for 'still'). But Moorish alcohol may quite well have been nothing but a distillation of flowers for scent, not drinking-alcohol. And of course Islam forbids the latter.*

6 *Distillation as such could well be Arab, though the Alexandrian Greeks of (say) the first century AD are more likely. Distillation for drink, probably north Italy after 1200.*

7 The pot still. The parts are a kettle in which to boil the distilland (substance to be distilled), a condenser and a receptacle for the distillate, corresponding to the stages of a 1.

8 Impurities, consisting of trace alcohols and other substances, that impart flavour and also cause hangovers. The more interesting the drink, the more uncomfortable the sequel.

9 Water. There being no chemical reason why the spirit should be diluted, and a sound economic reason against bottling and transporting water, perhaps some dim puritanical motive is at work.

10 A rectified spirit is one repeatedly or continuously distilled to a high degree of purity.

Minor Spirits

1 Caraway seed. Dill and coriander are sometimes used. Individual Danes flavour their akvavit with elder, cranberry and many other plants.

2 Ice-cold, neat, in small glasses holding no more than 1–1½ oz., down in one, with a lager chaser and accompanied by suitable food. Until recently there was a toasting ritual, especially in Sweden, but it seems that this no longer holds.

3 A Norwegian brand that, following a long tradition, has journeyed to the Antipodes and back in a ship's hold, crossing the line or equator a couple of times in doing so. It is supposed to pick up something from the motion and the temperature-changes.

4 Arrak or rum from Java. Also aquavit and miscellaneous wines.

5 A neutral spirit made from grapes or sugar-beet and flavoured with a herbal infusion, anise (aniseed) preponderating in Pernod's case, liquorice in Ricard's.

6 The herbal infusion (see previous answer) is made in alcohol. The herbal substances are thus perfectly soluble in alcohol, but they are insoluble in water and become suspended.

7 Greece and Cyprus. Ouzo. Flavoured with anise.

8 All Tequila is mezcal, but not all mezcal is Tequila. Mezcal is the generic drink, like brandy, Tequila is a place, a small town in mid-Mexico and the region round it, giving its name to the superior mezcal made there, like Cognac.

9 Tequila, Cointreau and lime-juice in a cocktail-glass with sea-salt round the rim. Lock your flick-knife away first.

10 Koumiss. Camel's milk will do at a pinch. Chig-Ge is the Mongolian version.

Scotch Whisky I

1 Whisky that has been distilled in Scotland. Not all these questions require deviousness or subtlety in the respondent.

2 Three years. In practice the time is usually longer.

3 From Irish and Scottish Gaelic 'uisge beatha', lit. 'water of life' (cf. eau de vie, aquavit). Later usquebaugh, whiskybae. The modern form is not recorded until 1746.

4 In efficiency, therefore economically. The patent still is continuous, turning out spirit as long as alcoholic wash is piped in. The pot still must be cleaned out and refilled after each run. In flavour, of course, the superiority is the other way round.

5 Unmalted maize (Indian corn, corn as seen on the cob) as well as malted barley.

6 If not from the drinker's imagination, then from the smoke of the peat fire, or often just peat-smoke and hot air, used to dry the malt before it is ground and fed into the mash tun to have its sugar extracted.

7 The method of malting the barley, the shape of the still and the method of heating it, the distilling temperature, the wood of the cask, the length of time in cask, etc.

8 It means that, like most malts on the market, the one concerned is the product of a single distillery. A blend of malts is a vatted malt, of which there are a couple of dozen on the market but none very highly regarded.

9 Lowland, Islay, Campbeltown (at the end of the Kintyre peninsula).

10 True. An easy mark all round to dissipate any rancour over q 1.

Scotch Whisky *II*

1 Chivas Regal is a blend. The others are single malts.

2 None. There may be a little more or a little less water, but everything else is there in the same proportions as before. Nobody really knows what happens in the cask.

3 In the 1880s the vineyards of Cognac were devastated by the vine-aphid (see Q Wine – Intermediate, q 4) and production of brandy, the prosperous Englishman's standard spirit, fell off disastrously. Scotch moved into the vacuum, though naturally not overnight.

4 3,000. Many go straight for export and are never seen in the UK.

5 A dessert drink or alcoholic dish made from Scotch whisky, runny honey and a liquor produced by soaking oatmeal or porage oats in water. Sassenach recipes substitute cream for the oatmeal liquor. A partial exception to the statement in the headnote that Scotch will not mix. Atholl is a Scottish dukedom and 'brose' is connected with 'broth'.

6 Traditionally, oak casks that have held sherry. Of recent years the supply of these has fallen off and distillers have taken to importing casks used to age bourbon whiskey in the US.

7 Queen Victoria, probably under the influence of John Brown, her Highland retainer. Her choice of tipple is said to have startled Gladstone, probably because of the violence it did the whisky. He was a good friend to Scotch, legalizing its importation into England in bottle in 1860.

8 The more malt, the better the blend. Good blends, not much more than 50 per cent grain. Inferior blends, up to 80 per cent. Blending is a secret process.

9 Whisky out of the still is colourless. The colour comes from the cask and from additives such as caramel, sherry and molasses.

10 Japan; precisely, the Suntory distillery in Hakushu. It produces nearly 100 million gallons of malt whisky a year, more than the whole of Scotland.

Whiskies and Whiskeys

1 Old Bushmills in the north of Northern Ireland, licensed in 1608. Its premium Black Label blend, 'Black Bush', has an unusually high proportion of malt whiskey in it.

2 A teaspoon (a true coffee-spoon is too small), over the back of which to pour the chilled cream on to the surface of the mixture of Irish whiskey, hot black coffee and (if wanted) sugar.

3 From Bourbon County in Kentucky Territory, as it then was, where the first stills were set up in the 1780s. For many years bourbon has been made in other parts of Kentucky and in other states, but Kentucky remains the Bordeaux, so to speak, of the trade.

4 (a) Corn (maize) principally, with some rye and barley.
(b) Casks of oak charred on the inside.

5 An American whiskey produced as the result of a fermentation partly set off by the residue of a previous fermentation. The best known is Jack Daniel's Tennessee whiskey, often inaccurately referred to as a bourbon, though it is indeed similar to bourbon in style.

6 Bourbon, Angostura bitters, sugar (plus a slice of orange and ice).

7 Washington and Jefferson, the first and third presidents. In each case the product was rye whiskey, and pretty rough too, it may safely be inferred.

8 John Jameson is an Irish whiskey, the others are American.

9 Purity, and consequent lack of any persistent flavour, therefore a readiness to be swamped in various mixtures. 'Dullness' would be my word. Of course, lack of after-effects is associated with purity.

10 Malt whisky imported from Scotland and blended with a local grain spirit. And yes, quite properly so called; blended Scotch is malt and local grain. The advisability of drinking such whiskies is another matter.

Port

1 Along the upper valley of the river Douro to the east.

2 In the middle of the fermenting process, before all the sugar has turned into alcohol, grape spirit is added to the wine, stopping fermentation and increasing the overall content of alcohol.

3 Not in Oporto itself but across the river in Vila Nova de Gaia. (Once called Portus Cale, whence 'Portugal'.)

ANSWERS to page 55

4 *A blend of wines from the best vineyards and of one exceptional year. It accounts for only about 2 per cent of total production, but is apparently the most profitable part of the trade. In other words the poor old consumer pays through the nose and no option, since no competing product exists.*

5 *(a) It is aged in an oak cask for two years only.*
(b) It slowly improves, becoming ready to drink after ten to fifteen years but continuing to improve thereafter. It also accumulates a crust or sediment.

6 *Stilton is the traditional answer, but some people think it and other English cheeses smother the port and prefer something milder, like unhung Brie or Camembert. This school would accompany Stilton with one of the types of port mentioned in the next question. (The practice of pouring any kind of port into a hole in a Stilton is regarded as being on about the level of brightening up caviare with a few dashes of vinegar.)*

7 *(a) A blend of wines from a single good but not necessarily vintage year aged in wood for about five years, bottled and ready to drink at once.*
(b) The same, made with wines of different years.
(c) A blend of wines from good but not necessarily all vintage years, to be laid down like vintage port, but cheaper.

8 *Just like all the other port, but with white grapes.*

9 *Equal parts of any old port and brandy. Supposed to be ineffective if the two are drunk successively. Many old stagers swear by it.*

10 *Dying like flies was the most noticeable. To drink at a sitting three bottles of old-style port, a light table wine, is one thing; to drink the same amount of the brandified article is quite another.*

Sherry

1 From a small area in Andalusia in south Spain to the west of the town of Jerez de la Frontera, formerly Xeres, the X denoting a 'sh' sound.

2 Falstaff, of course, in 'King Henry IV Part II'. The usual mark for getting it right, but five off for not knowing. Did the last bit inspire a famous beer ad?

3 'Dry', from 'seco', is the usual answer. But 'vino seco' was not a Spanish phrase at that time, and 'canary sack', also contemporary, was certainly a sweet wine, as wine normally was then. So there.

4 Nothing as far as I know. He was referring to R. B. Sheridan the dramatist, of whom he went on to say famously, 'Such an excess of stupidity, Sir, is not in nature.'

5 Barrels are ranked in tiers holding wines of different ages. When wine is taken for bottling from the oldest tier, that tier is topped up from the next oldest, and so on back. There are thus no 'years' in sherry.

6 'Flor' ('flower'). Native to Jerez and still an unexplained phenomenon.

7 Roughly: Manzanilla, Fino, Amontillado, Oloroso, Cream. Roughly because there are occasional exceptions like sweetish Amontillados and dry Olorosos.

8 Both, plus the drinker's concern for the state of his drink. Half a bottle is considered about right for one man and one session, and fino deteriorates very fast when the air gets to it.

9 Montilla is quite a strong wine but unfortified; sherry has brandy added to it.

10 (a) A drink of sherry, sugar or sweet liqueur (unless the sherry itself is sweet), lemon and pounded ice.
(b) A kind of overtrouser once worn by horsemen in the US. From the Polish 'szarawary'.

Madeira, Marsala and others

1 Wood. English 'material', 'matter'. When the Portuguese discovered the island in 1419 it was so thickly forested that a clearance fire is supposed to have burned for seven years.

2 That is the correct order. Malmsey is supposed to be the finest. However, when the Duke of Clarence was drowned in a butt of it in 1478 it was just another sweet white wine.

3 The label can hardly be contemporary, but it still might be telling the truth. If so, the wine would probably be marvellous. Madeira seems never to go over the top.

4 Prince Hal to Falstaff in 'King Henry IV Part I'. Another anachronism of Shakespeare's: Henry was all over before the island was even discovered. But it seems hard to care.

5 In west Sicily, the invention of an Englishman (of course). When based at Palermo in 1798 Nelson got to like it so much that he made it the official RN tipple for a time. Garibaldi called it 'a strong and generous wine, like the men who fight with me for freedom'.

6 In zabaglione, the delicious sweet of egg-yolks and sugar.

7 Málaga.

8 Well, natural sweet wine, and if you think that pouring spirit into an already strong wine is a natural proceeding, no doubt the name will strike you as admirably appropriate. But still a great drink.

9 Banyuls, a 'vin doux naturel' (see above).

10 No, not Nigeria – Australia. A dessert drink and mixer made from sweet white wine and brandy. Yalumba comes from an Aboriginal word meaning 'all the land around'. But Yalumba table wines, some of which are now available in the UK, are perfectly serious.

Cocktails and Mixed Drinks

1 *If you can, you have solved a mystery going back to 1806, when the word first reached print. No one has overturned the* OED*'s verdict, itself nearly a century old: 'A slang name, of which the real origin appears to be lost.' And yet any day now . . .*

2 *My own shot: A short strong mixed drink served cold. So for instance the Collins (see q 6), being long, fails to qualify, whereas the Sour, the same thing minus soda, gets in.*

3 *In 1920 Prohibition stopped the legal production of alcoholic drinks in the U S and all sorts of semi-potables were run up and passed off as gin and other spirits, so raw and foul that they had to be smothered with fruit, sugar, bitters, anything to hand.*

4 *All Manhattans contain a dash or two of Angostura bitters. The Sweet Manhattan (the usual variety) has sweet vermouth, the Dry dry, and the Medium a bit of both.*

5 *A short broad vertical-sided tumbler, preferably heavy. The Old-Fashioned is served with ice-cubes, and the breadth of the glass enables you to put enough in without piling them up above the surface of the drink and numbing your nose on them when you sip. Useful for any drink on the rocks.*

6 *Sugar and lemon-juice with ice, topped up with soda-water.*

7 *Champagne is the common denominator. The other ingredients are as follows:*
(a) Fresh orange-juice. From Buck's Club.
(b) Guinness. The mixture is also known as Bismarck.
(c) Fresh peach-juice – the Bellini.
(d) Angostura bitters, sugar, brandy – the (vile) Champagne Cocktail.
(e) Even worse, and so not asked for, gin – the French 75.

8 *(a) Rum*
(b) Strega
(c) Benedictine
(d) Drambuie
(e) Galliano.

9 *(a) Gin, lime-juice, sugar.*
(b) Brandy, Cointreau, lemon-juice.
(c) Vodka, orange-juice.
(d) Brandy, white Crème de menthe. A favourite of James Bond's.
(e) Gin, cherry brandy, lemon-juice, sugar. But there are a dozen different recipes.

10 *(a) Tequila, Galliano, orange-juice.*
(b) Vodka, Galliano, orange-juice.
(c) White rum, Blue Curaçao, pineapple-juice, coconut cream.
(d) As (c), omitting Curaçao.
(e) Scotch or bourbon, Amaretto.

Inventors and Inventions

1 Angostura bitters. Siegert worked in the hospital at the river-port of Angostura (which is Spanish for 'narrows'), not long afterwards renamed Ciudad Bolívar. His bitters were intended as a tonic and digestive remedy. See Aperitifs and Such, q 8.

2 The continuous or patent or Coffey still. Coffey showed his invention to the Irish distillers, who didn't want to know, then to Scottish or Scotch ones, who did. The Coffey still, not much modified, is used to this day for the making of grain whisky, gin, vodka and other spirits.

3 The continuous still. Stein came up with his invention five years before Coffey, but was superseded. His name may sound German to some people, but there have been Steins in England and Scotland literally as far back as 1066.

4 *The Kir (rhymes with 'beer'), an aperitif of Cassis blackcurrant liqueur topped up with white Burgundy. Félix — to give him his accent — was a mayor of Dijon, where Cassis comes from.*

5 *Absinthe, an infusion of wormwood ('Artemisia absinthia') and other herbs in alcohol. Not specially more harmful than other strong drinks, but thought to be, and banned in many places for many years. Once thought to be an aphrodisiac. The most successful brand was Pernod. Present-day Pernod is flavoured with aniseed.*

6 *Jean-Antoine Chaptal, Napoleon's Minister of Agriculture, authorized and encouraged it. He was faced with a glut of sugar-beet and a rash of under-strength wines.*

7 *Eugène Charmat, a Bordeaux chemist, in the last century. Sometimes called the Charmat process or method.*

8 *Bartholomew Sikes, an English excise officer, in 1816. The Sikes system is in process of being replaced by the percentage-of-alcohol-by-volume system, whereby 70° = 40 per cent. See Pousse-Café I, q 9.*

9 *Dom Perignon, cellarer of an abbey near Epernay, certainly had champagne-as-we-know-it going in France by 1700, but there is evidence to show that English importers had anticipated him in the 1660s. See Patrick Forbes, 'Champagne', 1977.*

10 *Martini di Arma di Taggia, barman of the Knickerbocker Hotel (where it was also or earlier known as the Knickerbocker Cocktail), NYC, 1910. Jerry Thomas, a California barman, invented the Martinez Cocktail, a different drink. Martini Rossi Ltd make vermouth. The Martini-Henry gives a different kind of kick, being a nineteenth-century rifle. John Doxat, in his 'Stirred, Not Shaken' (1976), puts the case for di Taggia most persuasively. Yet I cannot feel we have found out all there is to be found out of the matter.*

Pousse-Café 1

1 It crushes the grapes without also crushing the pips and releasing their unpalatable oils. Devising a machine to do the same proved not to be easy.

2 A burra peg. A 'peg' is nineteenth-century, mainly Anglo-Indian, slang for a drink of spirits, usually brandy and water. 'Chota' and 'burra' are Hindustani words for 'small' and 'large'.

3 A glass of Byrrh, a vermouthy brand of wine aperitif. Paris, because a waiter or barman there would be more likely to pretend wittily that he thought that that was what you wanted.

4 True. A cotton-gin is a machine for separating cotton from its seeds. But a gin-mill is punningly a drinking-saloon (US nineteenth century).

5 If you were there. Mascara (a different word from the cosmetic) is a wine-producing district of Algeria – but they probably export it all to Russia for blending.

6 A Dutch mixture of brandy, egg-yolks, sugar and flavouring. Improved when thinned by stirring in more brandy.

7 Ay is a village in the Champagne country whose produce is given the highest rating, and Ahr is the name of a small river in Germany round which they make red wine. So now you know.

8 Without going into Magyar grammar it can be said that the higher the number the sweeter the wine. The reference is to the number of baskets of overripe grapes added to the cask. Five is the maximum.

9 He devised the logical system of calculating alcoholic strength by volume. We in UK are now going over to it, abandoning our own illogical one: 40 per cent G–L = 70° Br. proof. (I said it was a small debt.)

10 'Saki', H. H. Munro (1870–1916).

Pousse-Café II

1 *Gamay Beaujolais is not from Beaujolais; it is a California varietal (named after the variety of grape) wine. Confusingly, the grape concerned is not in fact the Gamay as used in Beaujolais but a sub-variety of Pinot Noir.*

2 *Brandy. Though it produces a lot of sherry too.*

3 *(a) Moonshine. UK 1785, US 1875.*
(b) Hooch. US 1877, UK 1927.
(c) Poteen, potheen, 1812.

4 *From the town of Spa in Belgium, that gave its name to all the other 'spas'.*

5 *'Roomed', allowed (not artificially encouraged) to reach room temperature, in practice 63°–68° F. Most red wines do not release their full flavour when colder.*

6 *(a) USSR (UK and US jostling for second).*
(b) Italy.
(c) US.

7 *Lime-juice, to prevent scurvy, a prostrating disease caused by lack of vitamin C, result of a shipboard diet that lacked fresh fruit and vegetables. Hence 'lime-juicer' or 'limey', derogatory term for British person, sailor or ship.*

8 *Ostentation, yes, and keeping a down-market label out of sight of the guests, very much so, but also to aerate the wine, let it 'breathe' more than it can in the bottle and improve both bouquet and flavour. Fanatics say decanting even improves a fine malt whisky.*

9 *A kind of mull made with port, sugar and hot water. Attributed to Col. Francis Negus in the reign of Queen Anne.*

10 *Stephen Potter, founder of Winesmanship.*

Pousse-Café III

1 *Bacchus, Dionysus. Strictly, 'Bacchus' began life as another name of Dionysus. Dionysus was one of those gods that periodically die and come to life again. Could this be a symbolic reference to the hangover?*

2 *A solution of honey in water. Mead was popular at the court of Attila the Hun about* AD *450 and centuries earlier.*

3 *A spiced or medicated mead, said to be good with curries. Not I think commercially made nowadays, but popular with amateurs.*

4 *Oak, which is strong but porous and 'gives' the liquor something. This is not to say much, perhaps, there being several hundred different species of oak.*

5 *(a) 6000* BC, *round the Caspian Sea*
   (b) 1000 BC
   (c) 500 BC
   (d) AD *100.*

6 *One vine to one bottle is the rough rule.*

7 *Removing the liquid from the solid matter left after fermentation. Nothing to do with racking brains or tenants, but from a Provençal word meaning 'dregs'.*

8 *False, really. If the bottle is there at all it should be on top of or beside the refrigerator, waiting to be drunk on the rocks. Chilling the bottle locks up the sparkle. (Imparted to me years ago by the head of Perrier.)*

9 *Only (d) is a drink, the colloquial name of akvavit (from a word meaning a 'mouthful').*
   (a) is the Canadian jay,
   (b) are rolled gingerbread wafers, as you know,
   (c) are collectively a feature of Scottish musical style, a short accented note followed by a longer unaccented one,
   (e) is a wheel in a cotton-gin (see Pousse-Café I, a 4).

10 *G. K. Chesterton.*

Alcohol and Your Interior

1 *A dodgy question. Alcohol draws the blood to the skin, giving a 'glow' but accelerating bodily loss of heat, so overall it cools you. Anyway, avoid serious drinking before going out into the cold. Have a couple when you come back in.*

2 *(a) None. For a proof of the contrary, try spending a whole evening on vintage port.*
(b) None, but see a 4.

3 *Speed – a short sharp alcoholic shock is very drunk-making. Unfamiliar drinks – the body learns to tolerate ones it knows. Then vague things like your mood, state of health, etc.*

4 *All sweet drinks are bad. (People will usually have drunk them with a pudding or after a large meal, anyway having mixed their drinks earlier by switching from gin to sherry to table wine (say) and going on doing so with whisky or beer. Hence the 2 (b) superstition above.) Also smoking, bad ventilation, exertion such as dancing, fatigue from staying up late, rich food.*

5 *No, not at all. Alcohol 'depresses', reduces activity of, the nervous system, i.e. is a sedative, a relaxant. Nothing to do with psychological depression.*

6 *True. Some heavy drinkers eat little or no protein, thus starving the liver. You can get the same result by drinking no alcohol but eating nothing but boiled sweets, say.*

7 *False. The affliction is mainly hereditary. Gin notoriously relieves it (see Gin, a 5).*

8 *A glass of milk or tablespoon of olive oil will delay absorption and effectively slow your intake.*

9 *(a) Rest, a warm bath, fresh air, a mild alkaline like Vichy water, bread and honey (to raise blood sugar).*
(b) Fruit-juice especially if chilled, a cold shower, coffee, a hair of the dog, anything like a Prairie Oyster (brandy, tabasco, raw egg-yolk), any rich, greasy or spicy food, aspirin (hard on the stomach).

10 *From an emphatic form of 'total' current at the time (1830s) of the first such movement. A teetotal abstainer was pledged to take no alcohol at all, not merely to eschew spirits.*

Solution to question on page 83: You will find the intruder at the foot of the answers to q 9. No Sennacherib. He was King of Assyria in the seventh century BC and is mentioned in the Bible and a poem by Byron, but never had a bottle named after him.